# Gandhi and Charlie

Also Edited by David McI. Gracie

*Meditating on the Word*
by Dietrich Bonhoeffer

# GANDHI
## and CHARLIE

*The Story of a Friendship*

As Told through the Letters and Writings of
Mohandas K. Gandhi
and The Rev'd Charles Freer Andrews

## Edited and Narrated by
## David McI. Gracie

*1989*

**Cowley Publications**
**Cambridge, Massachusetts**

International Standard Book Number: 0-936384-74-3 cloth
0-936384-71-9 paper
Library of Congress Number: 88-36686

*The cover photograph from Richard Attenborough's film "Gandhi" is
used by courtesy of Indo-British Films, with Ben Kingsley in the role
of Gandhi and Ian Charleson as Charlie Andrews. We wish to express
our gratitude to Twickenham Studios and Alison Webb, Production
Coordinator.*

## Library of Congress Cataloging-in-Publications Data

Gandhi, Mahatma, 1869–1948.
    Gandhi and Charlie: the story of a friendship / edited and annotated by
David McI. Gracie.
        p. cm.
    Includes index.
    ISBN 0-936384-74-3. — ISBN 0-936384-71-9 (pbk.)
    1. Gandhi, Mahatma, 1869–1948. 2. Gandhi, Mahatma, 1869–1948—
Friends and associates. 3. Statesmen—India—Biography.
4. Nationalists—India—Biography. 5. Andrews. C. F. (Charles Freer),
1871–1940. 6. Missionaries—Great Britain—Biography. I. Andrews,
C. F. (Charles Freer), 1871–1940. II. Gracie, David McI., 1932– .
III. Title.
DS481.G3G2114 1989
954'.03'5'0922—DC19                              88-36686

*Cowley Publications
980 Memorial Drive
Cambridge, MA 02138*

# Acknowledgments

The idea for this book came from Cynthia Shattuck, my editor. I had originally approached Cowley with the intention of publishing a collection of Andrews' own writings, now out of print, but she soon persuaded me that the story of his friendship with Gandhi was even more important to tell. We worked closely together in developing and researching the book, and I owe a great deal to her imagination and insight in the weaving together of story and texts.

How pleasant it is to be able to continue this list of those who have helped in the preparation of this book by naming Horace Alexander, mutual friend of Gandhi and Andrews, now approaching his 100th birthday in a Quaker retirement home outside Philadelphia. Horace Alexander's step-daughter, Cecilia Sibinga, kindly arranged my interviews with him and loaned me his photograph of Gandhi with Andrews in the hospital in Calcutta. It was James Bristol, another Philadelphia Quaker, who encouraged me to make this contact.

I thank my friends, Charles Walker, Tresa Hughes, and Gary Klein, for lending me important books and source material; Premilla Hobbs, for helping me understand India better; Andrea Cohen and her daughter Heather, for cheerfully volunteering long hours at the word processor; the librarians at the Lutheran Theological Seminary in Mount Airy, for searching far and wide for Andrews' books. I would also like to express my gratitude to the Publications Division, Ministry of Information and Broadcasting, of the Government of India for making the complete works of Gandhi available. It is from that collection that we have drawn his letters and other writings.

I owe a great debt as well to Louis Fischer's *The Life of Mahatma Gandhi*, Hugh Tinker's biography of C. F. Andrews, *The Ordeal of Love*, and Benasaridas Chaturvedi and Marjorie Sykes' *Charles Freer Andrews: A Narrative*, all of which helped me to supply the book's narrative thread.

The adult classes of St. Paul's Chestnut Hill, St. Peter's in the Great Valley, and St. Mary's at the Cathedral listened as I shared Andrews' writings with them, and proved to me by their responses that his insights are still very relevant for Christian people today.

My greatest debt of all is to my wife, Shirley, who has patiently supported this project for over two years.

In the many selections from the writings of Gandhi and Andrews which follow I have tried to stay as close to the original as possible, although I have at times resorted to abridgement to avoid issues and personalities extraneous to the main theme of the particular chapter. Sticking with the original has meant keeping prases like "brotherhood of man," which we are now learning to replace with inclusive language. We should certainly give all such expressions here the broadest possible reading, for in Christ, Andrews wrote, there could be "no subordination of one race to another, or one sex to another."

*David McI. Gracie*
*Church and World Institute*
*Temple University*

*for John Jacob Weaver*

# Table of Contents

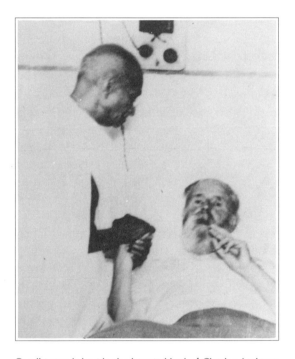

Gandhi stands beside the hospital bed of Charles Andrews

"Nobody probably knew Charlie Andrews as well as I did. When we met in South Africa we simply met as brothers and remained as such to the end."

—Mohandas Gandhi

# Introduction

This book is about a friendship, the rare, beautiful and enormously productive friendship of Mohandas Karamchand Gandhi and Charles Freer Andrews. Gandhi, the Mahatma or Great Soul, is known to millions for his leadership in the non-violent struggle for the independence of India as well as his attempts to rid India of the curse of "untouchability" and the painful strife between Hindu and Moslem. Andrews was an Anglican missionary priest who became Gandhi's closest Christian friend and co-worker. He is known to relatively few, even within the Anglican Communion, which might have some justification for regarding him as one of its own saints.

Whenever I talk to people who don't know about Andrews, I find the best starting point is Richard Attenborough's movie "Gandhi." With a little prodding of their memories, most people will recall the young priest called "Charlie" who appears on the scene in South Africa to lend himself to Gandhi's campaign for the rights of the Indian community there. You must remember, I say to my friends, the smiling chap with the clerical collar, the one who is helped up on top of the moving train by the workers who are riding there. "I'm going closer to God," he jokes. You certainly remember the sequence when Gandhi introduces him to non-violence with quotations from the New Testament, when they are being ordered off the pavement by some South African bullies. Charlie says, with a weak smile, that he has always taken those passages about turning the other cheek metaphorically. But Gandhi brings them through the sidewalk encounter unscratched. "That was lucky," says Charlie. "I thought you were a man of God," says Gandhi.

If you paid close attention to the dialogue you will remember

Charlie addressing Gandhi as "Mohan," and it is important to note that no one but Andrews shortened "Mohandas" to a nickname like that. There was a special intimacy between the two men that continued from their first meeting in South Africa in 1914 to Andrews' dying days in Calcutta in 1940, when Gandhi would visit him in the hospital and hold his hands while they talked of their shared hopes.

The Attenborough film captured some of that intimacy and something of the spark between the two men. But, for whatever reason, Charlie was removed from the film story before the first reel was over. He is last seen visiting Gandhi in an Indian jail, offering his services in a campaign on behalf of exploited peasant farmers.

"What do you want me to do?"

"Charlie, I think you should take that assignment you have been offered in Fiji."

Gandhi is sending him away. "I have to be sure," he says to Andrews, "they have to be sure, that what we have to do can be done by Indians alone."

"There are no goodbyes for us, Charlie. Wherever you are, you will always be in my heart."

This touching scene between Gandhi and Charlie Andrews serves to raise a genuine concern of Gandhi's that those non-Indians who helped the cause should not disempower the Indian people, who had to learn to help themselves. But it is a farewell that creates a false impression, since the close collaboration of Gandhi and Andrews was to go on for another twenty-five years, first in the campaign against indentured labor (which occasioned Andrews' trip to Fiji), then in the non-cooperation movement for Indian independence, their work on behalf of the untouchables, and more.

I don't think Charlie would have minded being blanked out of the rest of the story. I think he would simply have rejoiced that Gandhi's story was being told so well for the benefit of the coming generation. Andrews was shy and self-effacing. He played the same kind of role that Boswell played to Samuel Johnson; through his prolific writings he served as the interpreter of Gandhi to the English people, against whose empire Gandhi was waging his struggle of truth, his *satyagraha* campaign.

"They should have let Andrews become an elder statesman in the film," said Horace Alexander, a friend and co-worker of Andrews and Gandhi, when he allowed me to interview him at a Quaker retirement home outside Philadelphia. I had gone to see him in the hope that he could help me capture some sense of the two men and the quality of their friendship. Two notes emerged in what he told me that gave me a deeper understanding—he recalled their laughter at one another and he remembered Gandhi's desire for criticism.

"They liked to laugh at each other," Alexander said, when I asked him how they behaved together. In 1931 the three of them were in London where Andrews was in charge of arrangements for Gandhi's visit to the Round Table Conference between English and Indian leaders. "I remember Gandhi laughing at Andrews. He would jolly him about giving all his money away." Andrews was a good target for that kind of teasing, since he gave away his money, his overcoats—and once even a borrowed tea thermos—to whomever he met who was in need.

I brought up the issue of mutual criticism in the relationship because I had read this line in a letter from Gandhi to Alexander, a letter signed "Bapu," or Father. "I want you to criticize me as frankly and fearlessly as Charlie used to do." I suggested that Alexander might have filled the gap left by Andrews' death by being the trusted Christian friend who dared to be a critic too. Horace Alexander thought there might be some truth in that, but he told me that Gandhi really expected strong criticism from all his associates. In that respect, too, he thought the Attenborough film could be faulted for showing most people in Gandhi's entourage simply acceding to his wisdom and will.

Quite apart from any particulars gleaned in these brief interviews, it was enough for me to be with a man whose own writings revealed the same spirit as Andrews, a man who had been with Gandhi when India won its independence in 1947, and with Gandhi and Andrews together in the earlier years when the struggle for independence was being waged. I wanted his blessing for this project, and I think I received it.

Why, then, this story at this time? The ideal of non-violence seems to be in eclipse, at least in our land, and Charlie Andrews remains for us one of the best interpreters of the Gandhian non-violence movement. The history and philosophy of that movement need to be rediscovered by succeeding generations, just as Martin Luther King, Jr. rediscovered it for those of us who took part in the mass actions for civil rights in the fifties and sixties.

Racism is still firmly entrenched, both here and abroad, and the insights which Andrews gained about racism when in South Africa with Gandhi are of great value for Christian people. Andrews believed, to put it quite simply, that Christ died to overcome such divisions among us. That understanding of the Gospel needs to be offered anew.

A narrow fundamentalism is on the rise as well, with many Christians believing themselves compelled to win others over to a creed that does not recognize the working of God's Spirit in other religions. Gandhi tried to teach better things to the Christian missionaries of his day. We need to be confronted by those teachings again and see the way one Christian, at least, exemplified them.

The split between action and contemplation, between our work for social justice and a life of prayer, has reached a point where many of us are seeking to heal that unnatural and painful division in our lives. Gandhi and Andrews are remarkable models for that purpose: the most active of human beings, yet always centered in prayer.

Finally, we have much to learn about the possibilities of friendship from these two men, for friendship of the depth and intimacy they achieved is in short supply today.

The story of Gandhi and Charlie Andrews is told here, for the most part, in their own words, bridged by my own narrative and commentary. I present it in this way because Andrews wrote so well and so movingly that I think it is important to allow some of his writing to see the light of day again. Much of the narrative in this book is by Andrews; he was the scribe of the relationship, after all. But the letters, speeches and sketches by Gandhi presented here will be found to have their own immediacy and charm. It is Gandhi's presence that will loom largest, even though his writings do not.

Andrews wrote voluminously, chiefly about India and Gandhi at first, but then increasingly about his own life of action and prayer. His autobiography, *What I Owe to Christ*, is a spiritual classic; it tells us a good deal about his friendship with Gandhi as well as the life of prayer.

"Do you think it is God's call that your pen must be ever running?" Gandhi once chaffed him. "The world will not go to pieces for the suspension of your writing." But who was he to object? Gandhi's own works run to ninety volumes and fill several library shelves.

The focus of this book is always their friendship and the work they did together; the friendship forms, as it were, its spine. So we will look at those political campaigns and struggles and those religious issues in which they were both involved; we will read letters in which they expressed their love and concern for each other, and writings in which they explained one another and their friendship to the world.

Other important friendships of these two men will receive little notice here. This will inevitably distort the truth about them, because each had the gift of making a multitude of friends. Erik Erikson referred to Andrews as "the friend of the greatest of friends." But who was the greatest in this department is not easy to judge. Andrews' friends included the poet Rabindranath Tagore, assorted English bishops and viceroys, Hindu, Moslem and Christian saints and sages, young people around the world in the Student Christian Movement—and, of course, so many of the poor in India, Africa and Fiji. He sought them all out and bound them to his heart. Among his favorite words of Scripture were those of Jesus calling his disciples friends.

So for each of these men theirs was one friendship out of many, yet this particular friendship holds a special fascination for us, I believe. First, we are still surprised that such a friendship could flourish at all, because of the obvious barriers of color, caste, nationality and religion. Then we are amazed by its productivity. The pages that follow will show the energy of this friendship at work on many different fronts of social and political action. We are drawn to it, as well, because of its surprising quality of tenderness. Each of these two men had a strong mothering instinct, which expressed itself in the need to comfort and nurse the other in times of illness or stress. Andrews liked to be with Gandhi during his fasts; and in the letter which follows we can see how Gandhi would respond from his heart whenever his friend was ill.

¤   ¤   ¤

August 6, 1918

My dear Charlie,

I shall be good this time and not accuse you of crimes against the laws of God and man regarding health. But there is no doubt that you need a curator euphemistically called a nurse.

And how I should like to occupy that post! If you cannot have a nurse like me, who would make love to you but at the same time enforce strict obedience to doctor's orders, you need a wife who would see that you had your food  properly served, that you never went without an abdominal bandage and who would not allow you to overworry  yourself about bad news of the sickness of relatives. But marriage is probably too late. And not being able to nurse you myself I can only fret. I can do better if I pray and that is precisely what I am going to do. He must keep you well and free from harm so that you may glorify Him in your strength, if such be His will. . . .

With love,

Yours,

Mohan

◻   ◻   ◻

In telling others about the friendship, Gandhi once wrote: "It was love at first sight, when I saw him first at Durban." Durban, South Africa, is where the story begins.

# Chapter 1

## Two Seekers and Servants

**D**escribing his first encounter with Mohandas Gandhi in South Africa in 1914, Charles Andrews wrote, "Our hearts met from the first moment we saw one another." Before scanning the quarter-century of their work together, it might be well to search for the cause of that meeting of the two hearts. What had prepared the way for these men to become brothers?

Their differences were obvious enough: brown-white, Indian-English, Hindu-Christian. They were roughly the same age, in their early forties, but that was their only external similarity. It was their hearts that met; so we must look within to find an answer. Gandhi provides a clue, I think, in the tribute he wrote to Andrews after his friend's death in 1940. There he described himself and his friend as "two seekers and servants":

"Nobody probably knew Charlie Andrews as well as I did. When we met in South Africa we simply met as brothers and remained as such to the end. There was no distance *between us. It was not a friendship between an Englishman and an Indian. It was an unbreakable bond between two seekers and servants."*

*A brief sketch of their earlier years will indicate the nature of their seeking and who it was they wished to serve. Although they spent their formative years in two such different cultures, their similarities and common experiences are striking.*

*Each man was solidly related to the cultural and religious establishment of his time and place. Gandhi's family were hereditary prime ministers to an Indian prince; they were cultured and well-to-do Hindus of the merchant caste. Married to Kasturbai when they were both thirteen, Gandhi would leave family behind to travel to London in his nineteenth year to study for the Bar. In London he adopted British ways and a deep feeling of loyalty to the Empire. Then in 1893 a legal case involving a wealthy Indian merchant took him to South Africa, the country that would provide his first major arena of action.*

*Andrews studied and subsequently taught at Cambridge University. In his politics he was a fairly typical Empire loyalist, having absorbed that outlook from his father and others around him. His religious heritage was unusual, however, for his father was a minister in the Catholic Apostolic Church, the Irvingite sect, which combined elaborate liturgy with a vivid sense of the nearness of Christ's return. During his college years, Andrews turned away from his father's religion to the Church of England. This was not without pain, for the family was very close. By the time he was ordained a priest in 1897, he had become, as he would later put it himself, "a very narrow-minded high churchman." One of his teachers in the Anglican Church was the New Testament scholar Brooke Foss Westcott, Bishop of Durham—a man of wide and generous vision. It was Bishop Westcott who taught Andrews to look to the East for a more complete under-standing of Christ. Speaking "like an ancient seer, with a vision of the future before his eyes," Westcott would tell him that John's gospel, the gospel most loved in the English church, would someday be understood in a deeper and more spiritual way when Indian religious thought had been allowed to influence the Western Christian tradition.*

*Four of Westcott's sons had gone to serve the Church of England in India. When Basil, his youngest son and Andrews' best friend, died in India from cholera, Andrews decided he must go there himself and take his friend's place. So he left England to become a teacher in St. Stephen's College in Delhi in 1904.*

*A British-trained Indian barrister in South Africa. A Cambridge don who felt the call to teach in India. Their future lives seemed predictable enough within the British Empire of the turn of the century, yet each was to ex-perience a conversion which would change his life profoundly. We will let Andrews tell the story of what happened to Gandhi on the train at Pietermaritzburg, when he first faced the ugly reality of racism.*

¤　¤　¤

Gandhi, like Paul, comes clearly under the category of the twice-born among men of religion. He experienced at a special moment in his life that tremendous convulsion of the human spirit, which we call "conversion." In his early days he had followed a career at the Bar as a lawyer with great ardor. Success had been a main ambition—success in his profession; success in life as a man; and deeper down in his heart, success as a national leader.

He had gone out to South Africa on a business visit to act as a lawyer in an important trial, wherein two Indian merchants were engaged in litigation. Hitherto, he had only a distant knowledge of the color bar and had never considered what it might mean to himself if he was personally attacked and insulted. But as he journeyed from Durban and reached Maritzburg this dreadful experience came to him suddenly in its cruel nakedness. He was thrown out of his compartment by the railway official, though he carried a first-class ticket; and the mail train went on without him. It was late at night and he was in an utterly strange railway station, knowing no one. There all night long, as he sat shivering with cold, after enduring this insult, he wrestled within himself, whether to take the next steamer back to India, or to go through to the bitter end, suffering what his own people had to suffer. Before the morning the light came to his soul. He determined by God's grace to play the man. More humiliations were soon to be heaped upon him of the same character and in South Africa he was never without them. But he had put his hand to the plough and he would not turn back. . . . This was the turning point from which his new life would begin.

ロ   ロ   ロ

*The new life for Gandhi was one of identification with the oppressed among his own people. He organized and led the struggle of the small Indian minority (only three percent of the population of South Africa) against discrimination of all kinds. He founded the Natal Indian Congress and edited the paper* Indian Opinion. *In 1907 he began his* satyagraha *(truth force) campaigns, first against the pass laws, which required the registration of all Indians in South Africa, and subsequently against a poll tax that had the effect of binding Indian indentured laborers to unending servitude on South African plantations.*

*These campaigns of non-violent civil disobedience required of their participants a spiritual discipline which*

*Gandhi, his family and closest followers were to model in the communal life of the Phoenix ashram, which he founded in 1904. Gandhi's spiritual quest began and ended in the Hinduism into which he had been born, but it was influenced by the teaching of Jesus in the Sermon on the Mount. Gandhi was deeply impressed by the teaching of non-violence he found in the New Testament even while he remained largely unimpressed by the witness of most Christians he met, their claims to possess the final truth, and their intolerence of other religious traditions.*

*Tolstoy's Christian pacifist philosophy, especially in his book* The Kingdom of God is Within You, *affected Gandhi's thinking profoundly, while John Ruskin's* Unto This Last *crystallized his thoughts and led to the formation of the Phoenix ashram. Yet only the great Hindu scripture, the* Bhagavad Gita, *answered his innermost needs. As we read what Gandhi wrote about "the essence of Hinduism" in his mature years, we can sense how he sought to take an ancient faith and set it free to be more universal, more open to new truth. Truth was, in fact, Gandhi's name for God.*

¤ ¤ ¤

Let me for a few moments consider what Hinduism consists of, what it is that has fired so many saints about whom we have a historical record. Why has it contributed so many philosophers to the world? What is it in Hinduism that has so enthused its devotees for centuries? Did they see untouchability in Hinduism and still enthuse over it? In the midst of my struggle against untouchability, I have been asked by several workers as to the essence of Hinduism. . . . I have, for years past, been swearing by the Bhagavad Gita, and have said that it answers all my difficulties and has been my *Kamadhenu*, the Cow of plenty, my guide, my open sesame, in hundreds of moments of doubt and difficulty. I cannot recall a single occasion when it has failed me. But it is not a book that I can place before the whole of this audience. It requires a prayerful study before the *Kamadhenu* yields the rich milk she holds in her udder.

But I have fixed upon one mantra that I am going to recite to you, as containing the whole essence of Hinduism: the first verse in the *Ishopanishad*.

Now this mantra divides itself in four parts. The first part means, as I would translate: "All this that we see in this great universe is pervaded by God." Then come the second and the third parts which read together: "Renounce it and enjoy it." There is another rendering which means the same thing, though: "Enjoy what he gives you." Even so, you can divide it into two parts. Then follows the final and most important part: "Do not covet anybody's wealth or possession."

All the mantras of that ancient Upanishad are a commentary or an attempt to give us the full meaning of the first mantra. As I read the mantra in the light of the Gita or the Gita in the light of the mantra I find that the Gita is a commentary on this mantra. It seems to me to satisfy the cravings of the Socialist and the Communist, of the philosopher and the economist. I venture to suggest to all who do not belong to the Hindu faith that it satisfies their cravings also. And if it is true—and I hold it to be true—you need not take anything in Hinduism which is inconsistent with or contrary to the meaning of this mantra. What more can a man in the street want to learn than this, that the one God and Creator and Master of all that lives pervades the universe?

The three other parts of the mantra follow directly from the first. If you believe that God pervades everything that He has created, you must believe that you cannot enjoy anything that is not given by Him. And seeing that He is the Creator of his numerous children, it follows that you cannot covet anybody's possession. If you think that you are one of His numberless creatures, it behoves you to renounce everything and lay it at his feet. That means that the act of renunciation of everything is not a mere physical renunciation but represents a second or new birth. It is a deliberate act, not done in ignorance. It is therefore, a regeneration. And then since he who holds the body must eat and drink and clothe himself, he must naturally seek all that he needs from Him. And he gets it as a natural reward of that renunciation. As if this was not enough, the mantra closes with this magnificent thought: Do not covet anybody's possession. The moment you carry out these precepts you become a wise citizen of the world, living at peace with all that lives.

¤   ¤   ¤

*The second birth of which Gandhi speaks comes with the act of renunciation. The incident on the train at Pieter-maritzburg caused him to decide to renounce his pretence at status and his pursuit of individual gain in order to identify with his people in their struggle. An incident not long afterward moved him to identify more especially with the poor among his people. In his autobiography, which he called* The Story of My Experiments with Truth, *Gandhi tells of his meeting with a poor indentured laborer who came to him bleeding after a beating by his master, and stood before him, turban in hand, showing humble deference to the "sahib." Up until this time, Gandhi's work with the Natal Indian Congress had been exclusively among the merchants and the clerical class. He had wanted to win over the workers in the cane fields to the cause, but knew this could only be done by serving them. His opportunity now presented itself in the form of a man named Balasundaram.*

¤   ¤   ¤

I had put in scarcely three or four months practice, and the Congress was still in its infancy, when a Tamil man in tattered clothes, head-gear in hand, two front teeth broken and his mouth bleeding, stood before me trembling and weeping. He had been heavily belaboured by his master. I learnt all about him from my clerk, who was a Tamilian. Balasundaram—as that was the visitor's name—was serving his indenture under a well-known European resident of Durban. The master, getting angry with him, had lost self-control, and had beaten Balasundaram severely, breaking two of his teeth.

I sent him to the doctor. In those days only white doctors were available. I wanted a certificate from the doctor about the nature of the injury. I secured the certificate and straightway took the injured man to the magistrate, to whom I submitted his affidavit. The magistrate was indignant when he read it, and issued a summons against the employer. It was far from my desire to get the employer punished. I read the law about indentured labour. If an ordinary servant left service without giving notice, he was liable to be sued by his master in a civil court. With the indentured labourer, the case was entirely different. He was liable, in similiar circumstances, to be proceeded against in a criminal court and to be imprisoned on conviction. That is why Sir William Hunter called the indentured system almost as bad as slavery. Like the slave, the indentured labourer was the property of his master.

There were only two ways of releasing Balasundaram; either by getting the Protector of Indentured labourers to cancel his indenture or transfer him to someone else, or by getting Balasundaram's employer to release him. I called on the latter and said to him: "I do not want to proceed against you and get you punished. I think you realize that you have severely beaten the man. I shall be satisfied if you will transfer the indenture to someone else." To this he readily agreed. I next saw the Protector. He also agreed, on condition that I find a new employer.

So I went off in search of an employer. He had to be a European, as no Indian could employ indentured labour. At that time I knew very few Europeans. I met one of them. He very kindly agreed to take on Balasundaram. I gratefully acknowledged his kindness. The magistrate convicted Balasundaram's employer, and recorded that he had undertaken to transfer the indenture to someone else. Balasundaram's case reached the ears of every indentured labourer, and I came to be regarded as their friend. I hailed this conviction with delight. A regular stream of indentured labourers began to pour into my office, and I got the best opportunity of learning their joys and sorrows.

The echoes of Balasundaram's case were heard in far off Madras. Labourers from different parts of the province, who went to Natal on indenture, came to know of this case through their indentured brethren.

There was nothing extraordinary in the case itself, but the fact that there was someone in Natal to espouse their cause and publicly work for them gave the indentured labourers a joyful surprise and inspired them with hope.

I have said that Balasundaram entered my office, headgear in hand. There was a peculiar pathos about the circumstance which also showed our humiliation. I have already narrated the incident when I was asked to take off my turban in court. A practice had been forced upon every indentured labourer and every Indian stranger to take off his head-gear when visiting a European, whether the head-gear were a cap, a turban or a scarf wrapped round the head. A salute with even both hands was not sufficient. Balasundaram thought that he should follow the practice even with me. This was the first case in my experience. I felt humiliated and asked him to tie up his scarf. He did so, not without a certain hesitation, but I could perceive the pleasure on his face.

It has always been a mystery to me how men can feel themselves honoured by the humiliation of their fellow beings.

◻    ◻    ◻

*We see Gandhi, then, as one who understood himself to be a seeker after truth and a servant of the poor. The same can be said of Andrews, who also calls himself a twice-born man in this chapter from his autobiography entitled "The New Life in India."*

◻    ◻    ◻

A common word, *dwija*, can be found in most North Indian languages, meaning twice-born. In a very real sense I have been a *dwija*, because my life has been cut in two. Half of it has been lived in the West and half in the East. Any claim I have of being an interpreter between East and West comes from this source.

From the first day I landed in India, it became clear to me that I had entered a different world of human thought, fascinating and perplexing by its very unfamiliarity. Later on it was possible for me to learn much of the unity of human character which lay beneath all the difference. But the change of perspective at first dazzled my eyes.

After nearly thirty years of life spent in the East certain great facts in my own religious thinking stand out in the foreground. By far the greatest of these is this: that Christ has become not less central but more central and universal, not less divine to me, but more so, because more universally human. I can see him as the pattern of all that is best in Asia as well as in Europe.

◻    ◻    ◻

*As with Gandhi, we find in Andrews an ever-deepening loyalty to the religion of his birth and his people, yet he discovered in that religion a universality which frightened and alienated many who claimed the same loyalty. As his own vision of Christ expanded, everything in Christianity*

*that tended to exclude others offended him, whether it was
the Athanasian Creed, which damned those who did not
accept the correct trinitarian belief, or the practice of
European Christians, who enforced racial segregation even
at the table of the Lord. For Andrews, Christ would never
again be simply the God of the West.*

¤   ¤   ¤

Since I have learned to know Christ afresh in this Eastern
setting, it has been easy for me to point out the weakness of
his portraiture, when his character has been depicted with only
Western ideals to draw from, as though these comprehended
the "fullness of Christ," for in such pictures the true proportion
has not been kept. Some of the marked traits of his character
have not appeared at all. Much has been lost. Some day I would
like to draw his likeness anew with the color of the Eastern sky
added to the scene.

For the supreme miracle of Christ's character lies in this,
that he combines within himself, as no other figure in human
history has ever done, the qualities of every race. His very
birthplace and home, in childhood, were near the concourse
of the two great streams of human life in the ancient world,
that flowed east and west. Time and place conspired, but the
divine spark came down from above to mold for all time the
human character of the Christ, the Son of Man.

This is a tremendous claim to set forward. In all other ages
of mankind, verification would have been impossible, because
the world of men had not yet been fully explored. But in our
own generation the claim may at last be made and may be
seen to correspond with the salient facts of human history. For
those who through intimate contact with other races have
gained the right to be heard have borne witness that each race
and region of the earth responds to His appeal, finding in the
Gospel record that which applies specifically to themselves.

18

His sovereign character has become the one golden thread running through the history of mankind, binding the ages and the races together.

"Who is this Son of Man?" the different generations ask in turn. Apart from Jesus there is no human character that can embody adequately in his own person the full yearnings of mankind.

¤   ¤   ¤

*Here Andrews is describing the Jesus he had seen once in a vision while a college student at Cambridge, the One to whom he had been earlier converted in an experience movingly described in his autobiography,* What I Owe to Christ. *There he tells how God and Christ became one in his innermost thoughts, an equation he said he could not explain logically, but which he sought to illuminate with the use of the Indian word* rupam, *which means "form." The Formless One who ever seeks to take form did so in Christ, he found. For Andrews in that conversion experience, Christ became "God's* rupam, *God's word, articulate and intelligible to my heart." Could such a strong confession of Christian faith leave room for the effects of Eastern religions? In fact, his faith would be corrected and deepened by all that he learned in the East.*

¤   ¤   ¤

The main conception of God, which I had been taught in England to hold as true, was that of One who is the Creator and Ruler of all mankind. "I believe in God the Father Almighty, Maker of heaven and earth." Thus the Creed ran. The picture which I naturally drew for myself was that of Someone outside myself, infinitely great, who had fashioned the world by his power and was the Ruler over the kingdoms of men. My home training tended to increase the awe this conception carried with it. The only intimate word was "Our Father," and this brought me direct to Christ and his great love, taking away some of the fear.

But when I went deep into the heart of India, I found the whole emphasis to be laid on the realization of God inwardly and spiritually within the soul. There was no less awe than in the West, but it was of a more inward character.

This, when fully grasped, brought me nearer to Saint John's gospel than the ordinary Western teaching. It meant that not only Christ could say, "I and my Father are one," but that we, as God's children, in all reverence, could say this also.

The East regards the Eternal Divine Spirit—the *paramatma* moving within the soul of man—as spaceless and timeless, yet he ever uses "time" and "space" as a garment of self-revealment. He is unmanifest, yet he is mirrored by the pure in heart in the depth of the human spirit. He is invisible, yet he is visible in great human souls. He is formless, yet he takes form in man.

It is true that there are scriptures even of the Old Testament—such as Psalm 145—which come near to this inward view of God, but the general picture of the Lord of Hosts is more external. Again, in the writings of Plato we have the same ideas expressed in perfect Greek form, but Platonism has hitherto been unable to take deep root in the bleak climate of Northern Europe. Saint John, the Cambridge Platonists, the German mystics, George Fox and the Society of Friends— all these have found their joy in this inner light. But the West generally has believed in a transcendent rather than an immanent God.

In some such way as this I began to understand from my own personal experience that both environments of human thought—the Eastern and the Western—are needed to complete the portrait of the divine and human in Christ, just as two hemispheres of the globe appear to be necessary for the fulfillment of man's destiny on this planet.

Yet it was not any academic theory as to the difference between East and West, stated in general terms, which drove me as a Christian seeker after truth to face the new religious atmosphere as it came streaming in on every side. Much rather, it was the hard, concrete reality of everyday life in Delhi compelling me to face practical issues and to look carefully at each step of the way as I went forward, lest by any means I should fail to follow closely Christ, my Master, along these new and unfamiliar paths. With his guidance, after prayer and communion, I took one step forward after another, finding him indeed to be the way, the truth, and the life.

¤    ¤    ¤

*It was in the practical issues that Andrews distinguished himself from most other English missionaries and from other colonialists. For example, he succeeded in advancing his friend Susil Rudra to become the first Indian principal of St. Stephen's College. He supported Indian workers in strike situations and came to empathize so strongly with the needs of the Indian people that he was outspoken in the press for the full independence of India in advance of many others, including Gandhi himself.*

*The service of the poor had been axiomatic for Andrews from the time of his youthful conversion experience. Filled with his new-found love of Christ, he had gone immediately to visit people in a slum neighborhood he had overlooked before. Later, while preparing for ordination, he chose to work at the Pembroke College Mission among the poor of London. Like Gandhi, Andrews too would have a trans- forming encounter with an indentured "coolie" laborer in South Africa—an encounter that would direct his energies toward the ending of the indentured labor system within the British Empire.*

*The larger goals of these two men were clearly in har-*

mony, yet there were important differences between them. As we see some of these differences unfold in the pages that follow, we may ask to what extent they were the result of religion and culture, or simply of temperament.

Andrews had the temperament and outlook of an artist; his love for Rabindranath Tagore, the Indian poet, was one of the deepest of his life. For Tagore succeeded in delivering him from the negative, world-denying aspect of the Christianity Andrews had learned in England, teaching him to rejoice in all his senses. We get a feeling for what this meant to Andrews in these lines from a poem he wrote after reading Tagore's Gitanjali.

> Silent within the temple of the soul
> I worshipped, and beheld life's vision whole;
> No false mirage seen in ascetic mood,
> But as, when God first made it, very good,
> Each door of sense unbarred, and open all,
> To greet His advent and obey His call.

While Gandhi was a man of humor and love for all creatures, he was also an ascetic and stern prophet. That asceticism and sternness would not always sit well with Andrews, who claimed to find his friend a bit like St. Paul. He once wrote of Gandhi that his compassion went hand in hand with "a sense of the black horror of sin, especially the sins of the flesh; a severity towards those whom he loves most dearly, lest they should fall short of his own earnest longing for them, and yet withal a pathetic tenderness of heart which makes him long for the touch of human sympathy whenever he is misunderstood." Andrews, better than anyone else, would supply that touch.

Andrews badly needed sympathy and understanding as well. At times he felt driven to do more than was humanly possible and worried fruitlessly about the fate of his many friends, which subjected him to spells of physical and mental fatigue. It says much about the closeness of their friendship that Gandhi was able to learn how to minister to Andrews in his times of anxiety.

A further note of agreement in the religious outlook of the two friends, and one which will come up again and again, was the value they each placed on penance as a means of atonement. Whenever Gandhi undertook a fast, he was certainly bringing moral pressure on others to change their violent ways. In his own mind, however, he was also undertaking penance for that violence. Andrews would come to see in Gandhi a reflection of the suffering Christ, who takes upon himself the punishment for the sins of his people.

Gandhi similarly found in Andrews a penitent spirit. He saw Andrews living a life of penance for the sins of the British—somehow making up by his own patience and kindness for the arrogant behavior of the colonial rulers. It was this mode of life that enabled Gandhi to say to his followers that they could love the English still, because there were Englishmen like Charlie Andrews. The following aphorism is from Gandhi, but it could have come from his good friend as well: "I saw that nations, like individuals, could only be made through the agony of the cross and in no other way. Joy comes not out of the infliction of pain on others, but out of pain voluntarily borne by oneself."

With this sketch of the two friends' characters and beliefs in mind, we proceed to their first meeting in 1914 and follow the interactions of their lives over the years, allowing them to tell the story themselves as much as possible.

# Chapter 2

## South Africa

The S.S. Umtali, which was due to arrive on the 28th ult., was so delayed by heavy seas and head winds in the Indian Ocean that she was not sighted until early on the 2nd inst. The Indian community, who were awaiting the coming of the Rev. C. F. Andrews and Mr. W. W. Pearson from India by this boat, were feeling anxious at the delay.

*Thus began the lead story in Gandhi's South African newspaper,* Indian Opinion, *on January 7, 1914. Entitled "Arrival of Mr. Andrews and Mr. Pearson," the story reported the reception of the visitors on the dock by a representative group of Indians, both Hindu and Moslem, and European Christians.*

*Why had Andrews come to South Africa? Typically, it was an act of impulse. Gandhi had been leading a mass* satyagraha *campaign to force the removal of the poll tax of three pounds that had been placed on Indian indentured laborers whose contracted period of servitude was coming to an end. Since these workers in the cane fields were* penniless, the effect of the tax was to deny them any hope of freedom, forcing them back into a renewed period of indenture or a return home to poverty in India. Gandhi's campaign involved many thousands in illegal marches and had brought the coal miners out on strike. Among the thousands arrested were Gandhi and Kasturbai, his wife.

In Delhi meanwhile, where Andrews taught, public opinion ran high over the plight of South Africa's Indians. At one public meeting Andrews heard Gopal Krishna Gokhale, a respected leader of the Indian National Congress, issue an appeal for help, and his response to the appeal was total. He resigned his post at St. Stephen's, gave all his possessions to the cause, and boarded a steamer for Durban, accompanied by his close friend Willie Pearson. Gokhale was very pleased to have them go, hoping that they would be able to influence the authorities in a way that Indians had not been able to do.

In South Africa Andrews assumed the role he would so often play in the future—the wandering ambassador, factfinder, publicist, and source of inspiration in local struggles for justice. His departure from Delhi coincided with Gandhi's arrest, but by the time he arrived in South Africa, several weeks later, Gandhi had been released and was present on the dock to greet him.

Andrews had eagerly anticipated this meeting, describing his sea journey in a letter to a friend as "a pilgrimage to touch his feet." He looked for Gandhi when he landed but could not recognize him in the group from pictures he had seen, for by this time Gandhi had adopted the simple dress of the Indian coolie. He had to ask another member of the welcoming party to point him out.

¤   ¤   ¤

25

He pointed to an ascetic figure with head shaven, dressed in a white *dhoti* [loin cloth] and *kurta* [shirt] of such coarse material as an indentured laborer might wear, looking as though in mourning, and said: "Here is Mr. Gandhi." I stooped at once instinctively and touched his feet, and he said in a low tone, "Pray do not do that, it is a humiliation to me."

¤   ¤   ¤

*This touching of the feet was an Indian display of reverence. It apparently embarassed Gandhi and certainly shocked many white settlers when they heard of it. But that was Charlie's effusive way.*

*It was shortly after that public meeting that the personal breakthrough occurred, when Andrews' reverence and Gandhi's embarassment gave way to friendship. Andrews' biographers describe the moment when this happened. It was in the midst of a heated discussion about the correct negotiating stance to adopt with the Interior Minister, General Jan Christian Smuts.*

¤   ¤   ¤

The Indian leaders met, Andrews with them. After a few minutes talk he turned to Mr. Gandhi. "Isn't it simply a question of Indian honour?" he asked. Gandhi's eyes flashed. "Yes!" he said vehemently, "that is it, that is it. That is the real point at issue." "Then," said Andrews, "I am sure you are right to stand out. There must be no sacrifice of honour." He and Gandhi were friends from that hour; within two or three days they were "Mohan" and "Charlie" to one another.

¤   ¤   ¤

*Andrews spent the next six weeks with Gandhi, visiting and observing estates where Indian laborers were employed and working with Gandhi in his negotiations with Smuts.*

*He faced an impressive round of meetings as well, for the Indian community had great hopes that he would become their publicist and advocate at home in India. Here is one partial Sunday schedule as reported in* Indian Opinion.

¤   ¤   ¤

On Sunday at 2:30 p.m., Mr. Andrews visited the Lord Bishop of Natal. At 3:30 p.m. he preached to the Indian Christians. At 4:30 p.m. he lectured before a representative gathering of Hindus numbering 300 at the Hindu Young Men's Association rooms. He recited the message of Gurudeva Rabindranath Tagore in Sanskrit and urged the Hindus to observe their religion and to preserve the noble traditions of India. At 5:45 p.m. a reception was given under the auspices of the Anjuman Islam. Thereat the guest spoke of his friendship with distinguished Mahomedans. The chairman thanked Mr. Andrews for accepting the invitation and hoped that on his return to India he would do his best to put their position before the Indian public. . . . About 200 people attended this reception representing every section of the community. In the evening Mr. Andrews preached at St. Saviour's Cathedral.

¤   ¤   ¤

*The white newspapers afforded Andrews an altogether different kind of response. His touching of Gandhi's feet when he met him at the wharf, upset them greatly. In a letter to Rabindranath Tagore, Andrews describes the personal visit of one white editor.*

¤   ¤   ¤

I can still see him, holding up his hands in horror and saying, "Really you know, Mr. Andrews, really you know, we don't do that type of thing in Natal, we don't do it, Mr. Andrews. I consider the action most unfortunate, most unfortunate." I felt like a little schoolboy in the headmaster's study, waiting to be whipped!

. . . They boil over with indignation that I—an Englishman, mind you!—should have touched the feet of an Asiatic. When I remind them that Christ and St. Paul and St. John were Asiatics, they grow restive and say that things were altogether different then. If I go down the street talking with one of my new Indian friends, everyone turns around to have a big stare, and I am buttonholed afterwards by someone who tells me, "Look here, you know. This really won't do, you know. We don't do these things in this country." And when I say politely, "I am very sorry, but I do these things," they say, "But only think of the bad effect it has on the Kaffirs."

¤　　¤　　¤

*The closeness between Gandhi and Andrews, now firmly established, continued to grow during their work together for the rights of the Indian community. Gandhi assigned his son Manilal as a sort of aide-de-camp to Andrews. The following letter, written from father to son, expresses tender regard for his new friend. It begins with Gandhi scolding Manilal for eating spicy foods, which stimulate tamas (animality) in him.*

¤　　¤　　¤

I have had two letters from you. I am sorry I had no talk with you. No doubt, I was very much hurt that you ate chillies. It is possible that you will not feel the effects just now. But never forget that tamasic food cannot but have an evil effect. I am sure it will do you good in future if you discipline your senses. For all that I can see, there has been no spiritual gain to you through your experience of jail. You have a great need to cultivate thoughtfulness. It is a rare gain to have come into contact with Mr. Andrews. I should like you to take the fullest advantage of the occasion by preserving the utmost purity. So far, Mr. Andrews has expressed himself perfectly satisfied about you.

Keep an account of *every pice* [penny] you spend. Have no shame about doing any work for Mr. Andrews. You may even massage his calves. Having done so once myself, I know that he probably finds it agreeable. Polish his shoes and tie up the laces. You must not forget to write me every day. Maintain a diary of meetings with all persons and the developments from day to day.

> Blessings
> from
> Bapu

¤ ¤ ¤

*The critical bargaining session with Smuts took place on January 21, 1914 in Pretoria, less than a month after Andrews' arrival. At the time, Gandhi's wife was very ill as a result of her imprisonment. As Andrews tells the story of how the Draft Agreement was signed, he reveals the blend of the pastoral with the political which marked all his work.*

¤ ¤ ¤

One story of this period concerning Mahatma Gandhi and General Smuts is so beautiful that I must tell it before passing on to other events.

Of all the Indians who had suffered in prison Mrs. Gandhi had suffered most. I had tried to see her in jail, when I arrived in Natal, but she was too ill to see me. All the while when we were in Pretoria our anxiety about her health had been very great indeed. Then as negotiations proceeded she was released with all the other prisoners, but her health was broken and she got weaker everyday. We were not yet able to leave Pretoria, because some of the questions in dispute still remained unsettled and some deadlock might occur at any moment. Then all was agreed upon and the only thing left was to obtain General Smuts' signature to the Draft Agreement. We were warned however, that this might take several days on account of a syndicalist strike which demanded all his attention. Just then a telegram came to Mahatma Gandhi telling him that his wife was dying. I pressed him to start at once, leaving the final signature of General Smuts in my hands. But he refused. No public duty, he said, could be shirked for a private cause. He was firm as a rock,and I could not shake him; but I could see what his suffering was.

That night I could not sleep; and some time after midnight the thought came suddenly to me that I should go early to the Union Buildings and seek to obtain General Smuts' signature myself. This thought relieved my mind and I went to sleep. In the morning I reached the Union Buildings soon after six. For, while General Smuts was engaged in trying to check the strike he used to go for long journeys across the country each day, starting very early. At seven o'clock he came, and when I told him the news he was greatly shocked. His most human side came to the front in a moment and he asked for the Draft Agreement. He read it through and asked me if every point was included in it. When I answered "Yes," he signed it, and I had the great joy of hurrying back with it for Mahatma Gandhi. We went down to Durban together that very mornning, and on our journey by train the good news reached us that Mrs. Gandhi was better.

¤    ¤    ¤

*In June of 1914 the Indian Relief Act, based on this January draft, was passed in the Union of South Africa's Parliament. The passage of the Act, which ended the poll tax and provided for the phasing out of the indentured labor system, as well as giving recognition to Indian mar-*

*riages, was greeted by Gandhi as a victory. Here are his words, written at the time, celebrating the passage of the legislation and evaluating the factors which produced the victory, among them the "spirit" of his new friend, Andrews.*

¤  ¤  ¤

What could have contributed to this high tone of the debate? Certainly the watchfulness of the Imperial Goverment; certainly also, the courageous handling of the question by the Viceroy. Mr. Andrews' mission of love, too, contributed not a little to the lofty tone of the debate. His spirit seemed to watch and guide the deliberations of the House. And none of these helps would have been at our disposal if we had not helped ourselves. The spirit of Passive Resistance, it was, which made this trinity of causes possible. Let the community, therefore, understand that its last weapon at the critical moment is Passive Resistance, which has once more been fully vindicated. But we hope and we have reason to believe that the community will not be called upon again to pass through the terrible fire of suffering which it has had to pass through during the last, long years.

¤  ¤  ¤

*We can see that from the very beginning each man used the other as a paradigm. For Gandhi, at first, Andrews would exemplify what was best in the Empire, from which he expected support in his efforts for reform. Later, when the die was cast in the struggle for Indian independence, Andrews would become the example to which Gandhi could point when arguing for that love of the enemy—in this case, the British—which was so much a part of his philosophy of non-violence. For Andrews his friendship with Gandhi would serve to expose the lie of the dominant ideology of*

31

*racial and religious superiority, an ideology he wished to
root out and replace with the teaching of Christ.*

*Along with this symbolic function, their close working
relationship had great tactical advantages. The story of
Andrews' interceding with Smuts illustrates this well. At
the level of personal need, how else could Andrews have
become so involved in the action as he did through Gandhi?
For it was action he was seeking, not more years in the
lecture hall. He also longed to be admitted into the Indian
community, not as a "foreign" missionary, but as a member
of the family. When he arrived in South Africa, Andrews'
friendship with Tagore provided that entree; after South
Africa, it would be his relationship with Gandhi.*

*In his autobiography Andrews includes in his account of
the weeks in South Africa an intimate description of Gandhi
and his community of non-violent resisters. Here we sense
the wonder of Andrews' discovery of this man who became
for him both a hero and a friend.*

¤   ¤   ¤

In Mahatma Gandhi himself, whom I thus met in South
Africa for the first time, this sovereign power of winning
victories through suffering was apparent in every aspect of his
hard life of pain. To be with him was an inspiration which
awakened all that was best in me, and gave me a high courage,
enkindled and enlightened by his own. His tenderness toward
every slightest thing that suffered pain was only a part of his
tireless search for truth, whose other name was God.

Once I remember sitting down with him by the side of a
stream, on a hot day, near Pretoria in the Transvaal. I had been
arguing that since nature had contrived that the higher life
should feed on the lower, it could not be contrary to the moral
order of things for man to take animal life for food. He turned
on me in the moment and said: "Do you, a Christian, use that

argument? I thought you believed that the divine Lord had become incarnate, not to destroy life, but to save it; that the life of Christ found its truth in sacrificing itself for you and others. Is not the divinest thing of all to give life, not to take it?" His words revealed to me in a flash his own spirit, which ceaselessly gave itself to the last limit of sacrifice and found joy in so doing. In him, from the very first, I felt instinctively that there had come into the world not only a new religious personality of the highest order, moving the hearts of men and women to incredible sacrifice, but also a new religious truth, which yet was not new, but old as the stars and the everlasting hills. His one message was that long-suffering and redeeming love are alone invincible.

I found this in evidence throughout the whole South African struggle. The scene out there, among the small persecuted Indian community, reminded me of nothing so much as the early days of the Christian Church when the disciples of Jesus had everything in common. The first evening which I spent at Phoenix ashram, where Mahatma Gandhi and his followers had built up their own religious life together, revealed this. He was there, with the little children round him whom he loved. Mrs. Gandhi and her sons had not yet been released from prison and so he was there alone. One baby girl, belonging to an "untouchable" family in India, nestled in his arms, sharing her place there with a weak little invalid Muslim boy who sought eagerly to gain his special notice. A Zulu Christian woman had stayed for a while to take food with us on her way to the Zulu Mission on the hill. Every word spoken about the Boers and British that evening was kindly and even considerate. Again and again the words of the Acts of the Apostles came back to my mind, "They that believed were of one heart and one soul; and took their food with gladness, rejoicing that they were counted worthy to suffer for his name."

¤ ¤ ¤

*This conversation between Gandhi and Andrews is one that would continue throughout the years of their friendship. Gandhi's realization that "long-suffering and redeeming love were alone invincible" was not only to have a great influence on Andrews, but also to make him realize what his own Christian religion had in common with other faiths. It was the South African experience, the indenture struggle with its assumptions of racial superiority and inferiority, which brought to a head for Andrews the fundamental contradiction between racism and the gospel of Christ.*

*Yet at the same time he lived and served as a missionary of the Church of England, which in much of its practice was racist and whose doctrine condemned all those outside the Christian faith—which would include most of his new Indian friends. As we will see, in some ways his struggle with this evil would anticipate Gandhi's wrestling with the whole question of untouchability, its deep cruelty and divisiveness, as a fixture of orthodox Hinduism.*

*It was Gandhi himself who would provide the litmus test for the church on the question of race in Andrews' eyes. The Christian church in South Africa failed this test badly when first Gandhi and then his son Manilal were excluded from attending services during Andrews' visit.*

¤   ¤   ¤

At one of the Christian churches where I had been asked to preach, Willie Pearson had brought Mahatma Gandhi to the church door because he wished to hear my sermon. Afterward I found, to my utter shame, that the churchwardens had refused him admission, because he was a "colored" man and an "Asiatic." In such an act of refusal I felt that Christ himself had been denied entrance into his own church, where his name was worshiped. Those who knew the facts best told us that such things were constantly happening in South Africa. On a later occasion I had gone down to Cape Town, where the color prejudice is not so great as in Natal. Mahatma Gandhi had sent his son Manilal with me to look after my personal needs and he had done for me many kindly acts of service. The lad had become almost like a son to me, and one day he asked me eagerly whether it would be possible for him to come and hear me preach. So I took him to a suburban church, where the vicar was a great friend of the Indian community and the church itself had for a long while supported foreign missions in India.

We went to tea with the vicar and his wife before the service, and everything went well, until I suggested that Manilal should come to church to hear me preach. Then the vicar's countenance fell. For though he would gladly have welcomed it himself, his congregation might object. To have an Indian boy sitting side by side with them in church to hear Christ's message was almost an impossibility for them. A compromise was reached at last whereby Manilal, seated by the vicar's wife near the door in the back seat, was able to hear the gospel.

¤ ¤ ¤

*Some of the finest writing Andrews produced, with the most relevance for us still today, was in those essays in which he reflected on the racism he discovered in South Africa and then brought to bear upon it the uncompromising standard he found in the biblical witness.*

¤ ¤ ¤

We soon found out that the root of the whole mischief in South Africa was the race and color question. The one desire on the part of the Europeans generally in South Africa who were not actually sugar planters, was to get rid of the Indians altogether in the country as a "colored" race. They regretted that they had ever been brought over here. So long as they remained in South Africa they were determined to keep them in an inferior position, as "colored" people, subject to all the social and political disabilities of other "colored" races.

It seemed to me an impossible position to observe, as Christians, racial and color discriminations in human life. This would inevitably lead to a new caste system. Such a thing could never be the will of Christ, my Master, who taught the Fatherhood of God and the brotherhood of man. If Christendom ever finally became divided into "racial" churches, with a color bar standing between, and the sacrament of the Holy were denied to Christians solely on the ground of color and race, then this fundamental principle of the brotherhood of man, for which Christ died upon the cross, would be made of no effect. We should "crucify the Son of God afresh and put him to an open shame."

It was clear to me also from the New Testament that at Antioch Paul the apostle had withstood Peter to his face on this very issue, at a time when racial exclusiveness threatened to divide the Christian Church into two sections. This was the underlying basis of Saint Paul's great controversy, running through all his epistles.

Thus probably on no issue was the New Testament more explicit and the teaching of Christ himself more plain, than on this. "In him," Saint Paul writes, "there is neither Greek nor Jew. . . . barbarian, Scythian, bond or free: but Christ is all, and in all."

Yet when I reached Natal I found a racial situation within the church almost exactly parallel to that against which St. Paul had so vehemently contended. For "race" churches were actually springing up, and the color bar was being imposed on Christian people, not only by administrative acts but even by direct legislation. Social segregation of races was taking the same course and molding public opinion.

In certain respects this was an evil heritage from the past. For there had been a bad debt left over from the Boer Republics, whose *Grondwer* or fundamental law, had run, "There shall be no equality between white and black either in Church or State." The British settlers in Natal had instinctively taken up an attitude which was leading to the same results.

From the first day when we landed in Durban the racial prejudice was glaringly apparent. Soon we experienced it personally in some of its worst forms. It is an evil which is like a poisonous infection spreading over an otherwise healthy body. The infection had already begun in South Africa and there was very little effort being made to stop the disease. The Christian Church, in some of its branches, was itself infected.

¤     ¤     ¤

*Andrews, who had studied the New Testament with the finest scholars in England, now came to read its message in a new way, beginning with the teaching of Christ in the gospels.*

¤     ¤     ¤

It was astonishing to me to find what new light came to me as I faced those South African problems. For I was confronted by the very same questions of racial and religious exclusiveness which so deeply offended Christ and called forth his severest condemnation. I could see now exactly why Jesus had deliberately taken the despised Samaritan in his parable as an example to the godly Pharisee. I could understand how he had shocked the Pharisees still more by declaring that the publicans and sinners went into the kingdom of heaven before them. And there was a point that had strangely escaped my notice hitherto, in spite of years of study of the gospels at Cambridge.

Christ himself, with all the reckless courage of youth and with the power of God in his heart, had risked his life in his own village among his own people over this very question. For he told them at Nazareth how Naaman the Syrian and the widow of Sarepta—two people who were not Jews at all, but Gentiles—had received God's special grace in preference to the Jewish people.

Here, in South Africa, I could easily understand how such a daring outbreak as that had led to serious consequences. We read, "When they heard these things, they were filled with wrath, and rose up, and thrust him out of the city, and led him unto the brow of the hill whereon their city was built, that they might cast him down headlong."

The first disciples of Jesus, starting with all their racial and religious prejudices—such as I saw around me on every side in South Africa—had felt instinctively the Divine Spirit in Christ breaking through these narrow limitations and they had followed their Master step by step, eradicating one prejudice after another from their own lives. They watched him closely and saw how his heart went out in love to the Samaritan, the Roman centurion, the Syro-Phoenician woman, who were supposed to be outside the covenant of God's mercies and alien to God's grace. They had to learn that God's way of thinking was exactly the opposite of their own foolish racial way: that he loved these people all the more, not less, just because they had not received any special privilege and were looked down upon by others.

¤　　¤　　¤

*Of course in South Africa those most looked down upon by the ruling minority were the Blacks, the majority race. It would be well to remember at this point one criticism that has been made of the Indian political movement in South Africa: it never reached out to form an effective alliance with Blacks. Even Gandhi, who in his philosophy and in his own heart excluded no one, has been criticized for not doing more to achieve such unity.*

*It is in this context that the following account should be read. Here Andrews tells of a question directed to him by a Zulu leader shortly before he left South Africa in February, 1914. The question was: "Are you ready to die for us?"*

¤　　¤　　¤

A farewell meeting had been arranged for me by the Indian community in Durban, and I noticed that a large number of Zulus were also present. This had happened before, and I had marked the grave dignity of their bearing and the sadness written on their faces as they watched me speaking. On this last occasion I had gone back to the shop of an old Muslim named Mian Khan, where I was living, and had just sat down with him to tea. Two Zulu leaders entered and we invited them to sit down with us. Then one of them, pointing to me, said to Mian Kahn, "We want to ask him a question."

When this was interpreted to me, "Do please," I said, "tell me quite freely what is in your mind."

"We have seen," he answered, turning to me, "by the look in your eyes, when you speak to the Indians, that you are ready to die for the Indians. Are you ready to die for us?"

This simple question was asked with a wistful earnestness that went direct to my heart. I hesitated before answering, in order to speak with entire sincerity, and then said, "Yes, if the time comes, I am ready." For it came to me like a flash, while I paused, that in Christ's service there can be no thought of race at all; for all are one man in him. There can only be one divine love wherein all the races of mankind are one.

¤　　¤　　¤

39

*Notions of religious superiority and exclusion based on creed troubled Andrews also. The prayer book in use at that time in the Church of England still required the occasional recitation of the Athanasian Creed, which begins with these words: "Whosoever will be saved, before all things it is necessary that he hold the Catholic Faith, which Faith except everyone do keep whole and undefiled, without doubt he shall perish everlastingly."*

*The teaching still current in English theological colleges about the millions in India and Africa "perishing in heathen darkness" was abhorrent to him. Again, his association with Gandhi brought the question to its sharpest focus.*

◘    ◘    ◘

Not I alone, but numbers of sincere and earnest Christians in South Africa, when they watched the self-sacrificing conduct of Mr. and Mrs. Gandhi, would say with conviction, "These good people are better Christians than we are." Such words were not a mere formal mode of speech, but, rather, a direct acknowledgement of a divine truth, for these Indian passive resisters *were* better Christians, though they remained Hindus just as they were born. Facts like these had to be taken into account in reading the New Testament and in framing any theory of the Christian faith.

◘    ◘    ◘

*Andrews was coming to the decision that he could no longer serve as a missionary priest. He discussed this with Gandhi, who showed great understanding of his predicament and said that he was sure that Charlie would find a "wider sphere of Christian service." When, in August, 1914, Andrews wrote his bishop, renouncing his ordination vows, Gandhi thought of Andrews' father and the pain this decision might cause him. John Andrews was alone now—*

*his wife died while Charlie was in South Africa—and he was very ill. Gandhi wrote him these lines.*

¤　　¤　　¤

Charlie has been writing to me. . . . You are likely to be grieved over his having given up the clerical robe. I hope however that such is not the case. His action is no change; it is, I feel convinced, expansion. He preaches through his life as very few do, and he preaches the purest love. . . Charlie has evidently a mission {of} whose extent even those who are nearest him have no conception. May I plead for your blessings to Charlie in all his work? It will be such a comfort to him to know that nothing he has done has grieved you.

¤　　¤　　¤

*The best conclusion to a chapter highlighting the meeting of the friends in South Africa and those events which set the tone of their future relationship may be an excerpt from a goodbye letter written by Andrews to Gandhi on February 26, 1914.*

¤　　¤　　¤

It was so like you to be occupied in dear acts of service for my voyage. I didn't quite know how much you had learnt to love me till that morning when you put your hand on my shoulder and spoke of the loneliness that there would be to you when I was gone. When I saw you on the wharf, standing with hands raised in benediction, I knew—as I had not known, even in Pretoria—how very, very dear you have become to me.

# Chapter 3

## "What I Owe to Christ"

**W**hen he returned to India, Andrews finished his
duties at St. Stephen's College and then took up
residence at Santiniketan, the ashram of Rabindranath
Tagore in Bengal. This center of meditation and religious
culture served as Andrews' base for a number of years, a
place to touch down and recuperate. In What I Owe to Christ
he says of it: "There at Santiniketan I learned to understand
the spiritual beauty which underlies Indian life, keeping it
sweet through all the ages in spite of cruelties and wrongs
which have gone unredressed." The ashram would be his
resting place from travels around the British Empire and
his work with Gandhi, enabling his life to follow a pattern
of alternating work and contemplation. Now it was the
place where he was able to ponder the nature of his calling.

Gandhi also returned to India that same year and started
his own ashram at Sabarmati, near the textile-making town
of Ahmedabad. It was a quasi-monastic community where
personal possessions, foreign cloth, and spicy food alike
were forbidden. Even more striking was the fact that "un-

touchables" were included as part of the community. Andrews visited Sabarmati and was delighted to find the same commitment to serving the poor that had so impressed him at the Phoenix ashram in South Africa.

Yet he was quick to argue with Gandhi about the vows which those who joined in the community were required to take. At a time when he was renouncing his own ordination vows (or trying to! His bishop had wisely refrained from acting on his request), the whole notion of vow-taking seemed wrong to him. Andrews was particularly opposed to a vow of celibacy. Single himself, he had the strongest objection to prescribing for others an "empty, attenuated, emasculated life experience"—and he didn't mind telling Gandhi so in just those words.

In the summer of 1915, after a quiet time of readjustment followed by a serious bout with cholera, Andrews decided on the next step in that wider mission which Gandhi predicted for him in the letter to his father. It would be an effort to end the system of indentured labor, not only in South Africa, but throughout the British Empire. He would wage this struggle with Gandhi's help, and he would win.

Indenture is an evil that has largely been forgotten today, yet it had served to perpetrate human slavery in another guise in the British Empire long after the well-known work of William Wilberforce and the other Christian abolitionists had been completed. Here is Andrews' own description of how the system worked.

¤   ¤   ¤

The history of the first emigration of Indians abroad in large numbers, which happened just a hundred years ago, is full of tragedy. The humiliation of it can never be forgotten by those who love the good name of their country.

For when slavery was finally abolished in 1833, a crisis followed in the colonies where slave labor had hitherto been employed. The emancipated slaves refused to go back to work on the sugar plantations because this labor carried with it still the old stigma of slavery. Therefore, in order to save the sugar industry from extinction, the Governor-General was induced to allow indentured labor to be recruited in Indian villages for the colonial sugar plantations. Mauritius was the first colony to receive this Indian labour, in 1835. After this the system spread to other colonies also. Thousands of Indian villagers were sent out year after year. They were dispatched in what were called "coolie" ships to all parts of the world.

The immoral conditions under which they lived in their barracks, called the "coolie lines," were appalling. This was due to the extreme disproportion of women and the lack of married couples. Sexual jealousies arose. Suicides and murders were frequent. All the brutalities of the old slave days reproduced themselves wherever the employer himself was a hard taskmaster; for he had almost unlimited power. Adequate government inspection became practically impossible. Labourers who suffered from bad treatment were terrorized into silence.

There were good masters as well as bad. Under the former the labourers' lot was often a happy one. Many also settled down in the colony after the indenture was over. But the accumulation of misery and moral evil was immense.

That such a system—inevitably carrying with it the old stigma of slavery—should have been imposed upon India by Great Britain, so soon after the slave traffic was abolished, and should have gone on for over eighty years, shows very plainly indeed in what low esteem Indians were held.

¤ ¤ ¤

*Andrews' work in ending indentured labor in the Empire has been called his greatest single political achievement. It began with a vision, inspired by the memory of a terrible sight during one of his early days with Gandhi in Natal.*

¤   ¤   ¤

The next morning I was to see with my own eyes something of what was occurring under the indenture system in Natal in spite of all government inspection. While I was walking with Mahatma Gandhi, we saw the figure of a man crouching near the sugar cane. He drew close and touched Mr. Gandhi's feet and then pointed to some unhealed wounds across his back which had evidently been inflicted by a lash. He had run away and had now come to seek for protection. At first sight of him I had been slightly behind Mahatma Gandhi and now came forward to examine the wounds. When he saw that I was European, he suddenly started back with fear, as though I might strike him; and it was necessary to reassure him that I was not an enemy but a friend. That look of fear on his face as he saw me coming toward him haunted me for many days and filled me with pity.

¤   ¤   ¤

*The incident was to remain with Andrews for a long time. When he was recovering from the attack of cholera in July, 1915, he would see the same man again in a waking dream.*

¤   ¤   ¤

At Simla, I used to lie in a sunny veranda all day long scarcely strong enough even to read.

There had come into my hands, however, a Blue Book on Indian indentured labor which had a special interest for me because of what I had seen in Natal. While glancing through it and turning over the pages, I saw some truly appalling statistics concerning the suicide rate of Indians under indenture in Fiji. The Fiji islands were right out of the way, in the South Pacific, and it appeared from the report that owing to these demoralizing conditions, accompanied by homesickness, the number of suicides each year was almost incalculably in excess of those in India, among the same agricultural class.

Then the suicide statistics were compared with those of Natal and other places where Indian indentured labour was sent out, and the difference at once was startling. The misery of indenture in Natal I had seen with my own eyes, so that I was able to judge the misery of Indians in Fiji. I closed the book, for I had very little strength even for reading, but the thought of what I had seen in print obsessed me.

Some time after this, one day about noon time, I was lying on the couch in the veranda. In front of me, very clearly indeed, I saw a vision of that poor Indian labourer in Natal when he shrank back from me with his back torn and bruised. He was looking toward me now in a most piteous manner. As I watched him with great sorrow his face changed and I saw instead the face of Jesus, the Good Shepherd, which I had loved and known from childhood days. The image was so clear that my whole heart went out in reverence and worship. As I lay back there, it was some time after the vision had faded before I realized that it had been a waking dream, created by my own intense imagination and objectively thrown outside me by my subconscious mind.

The effect upon me was in a certain sense the same as if it had been a vision of the Lord himself. We use these terms "objective" and "subjective," and we are obliged to do so; but the border-line between them must often be very thin, almost to a vanishing point. It was as clear to me as daylight that Christ was calling me to go out to Fiji, and that his call would be fulfilled. It came to me, without any question now, that this thing had to be done. So I began at once setting about the task of finding what was the best route to go by, and how long it would take. This thought gradually got firm hold of me, and helped me to get back my strength, for it had given me new hope and a new purpose.

¤    ¤    ¤

*Andrews traveled twice to Fiji, in 1915 and 1917, accompanied on his first trip by Willie Pearson. These were fact-finding missions to observe and document the wretched conditions of Indian men and women there. Andrews used these findings to negotiate directly with Sir Edwin Montagu, Secretary of State for India, to put an end to this inhuman system. While Andrews did this work, Gandhi kept up the pressure of public opinion in India, threatening to instigate a campaign of* satyagraha *such as he had led in South Africa.*

*In Andrews' account of his work in Fiji we see how the visionary call led to the hard work of building political pressure to effect legislative change.*

¤    ¤    ¤

When we reached Fiji, we found that things were even worse than we had anticipated from the Blue Book account. More than anything else the condition of the poor Indian women under indenture was pitiable in the extreme. The very same moral evils existed, in what were called the "coolie lines," that had been notorious in Natal. But in Fiji the moral evil had gone far deeper. Since Indian men and women had gone out in thousands to different parts of the world as far distant from one another as Fiji, Mauritius, Natal, and British Guiana, and since a large yearly recruitment by professional recruiters in India was still being carried on, it was clearly time that the whole system should be brought to an end. I saw this clearly.

Though it was extremely difficult for the planters themselves to see this point of view, the Indian government felt the force of public opinion in India, and Mahatma Gandhi, together with Pandit Malaviya, made "Abolition" the principal political issue. The ladies of India took up the cause of their sisters in these far off lands. Lord Hardinge, as viceroy, accepted the evidence which we had collected in our report, and this helped to turn the scale in favor of a great reform measure, called the "Abolition of Indenture."

This abolition act was passed soon after the publication of our report in India on our return from Fiji. The facts which we brought back, concerning the terrible moral conditions on the plantations were so convincing that the viceroy had no difficulty in gaining the consent of the secretary of state for India to proceed with the Abolition Act in its final stages as soon as possible. But a modification was included at the request of the Colonial Office, which caused us much misgiving. For it was stated, that "some delay would be needed" in order to bring about the necessary adjustments.

In the universal rejoicing over the passing of the Abolition Act, this single clause was almost overlooked. Yet its effect was so serious that it involved the reopening of the whole issue a year later, for we discovered that an agreement had been reached in London to continue recruiting for five years more while adjustments were being made, and during that period to devise some other system which would bring back "indenture," only under another name. This could not be countenanced for a moment now that the evils had been openly acknowledged. Therefore the struggle was renewed. The Indian leaders asked me to go out once more to collect further evidence, so that no loophole might be left for the renewal of a curse which had already done untold moral harm and stirred up bad blood between India and Great Britain.

On this occasion I had to go out entirely alone, and during a stay of nearly a year in the South Pacific I suffered much from ill health and encountered far more serious hostility than Willie Pearson and I had done on our former visit. It was a time of very great depression and spiritual loneliness, with little of the joy I had experienced on the first visit. Yet the result of this visit was much greater than that which went before; for the evidence which I brought back this time was so overwhelming that practically no defense was possible.

◻    ◻    ◻

*After returning from the second visit to Fiji, Andrews had occasion to report to a meeting at Ahmedabad. Gandhi introduced him with words that let us see how he valued Andrews' work, and even more, Andrews himself.*

◻    ◻    ◻

I have had occasion before now to introduce Mr. Andrews to you. He can best be described as a *rishi*, for he has all the qualities of a holy sage. He has recently returned from Fiji, where he went on a mission that concerns us. While in Fiji, he did not put up in any hotel or with any well-to-do person; he lived among the labourers, in their own houses, and studied their manner of living.

It was I who advised him to go there to observe things, lest a system as harmful as indenture come to replace it. The hospitals Mr. Andrews [observed] are in fact no hospitals but engines of oppression, as one might say, for the plight of Indian women in these hospitals is miserable indeed. When Mr. Andrews asked the Government to open hospitals for women in that country, it replied that it was for the planters to do so, and the latter, on their part, said that the Government would attend to the matter when the system of indenture had ended.

In schools, children receive instruction in the Christian faith from the very start. This is not good for Hindu and Muslim children. Moreover, the education is through the medium of English and, therefore, our people gain little from it. The same thing obtains in Natal. Indian teachers are not available there, nor in Fiji. We can be of help in this matter. If a few men who will be satisfied with a small income go over to these places as teachers, that will be some help. One may also help by giving anything from a *pice* to a hundred thousand rupees. I don't know how to estimate the value of all these services of Mr. Andrews. He is a man of retiring disposition and service to others in his one mission in life. I have deliberately called him a *rishi*. A great man like him, given to serving others, we cannot thank enough.

¤　¤　¤

*A good sample of Gandhi's propaganda during the aboli-
tion campaign is found in the following article, which he
wrote in 1919. It contains a succinct statement of his
position on the issue of law and morality: "A law contrary
to morality is no law." It ends with an equally succinct
tribute to his friend.*

¤　¤　¤

A number of issues are involved in the Fiji problem but, for educating public opinion at present, it is essential to know only one thing. To speak plainly, indentured labour means a state of semi-slavery. The outrages committed on the womenfolk of the indentured Indian labourers have been possible simply because of our lethargy or, maybe, our ignorance. We have before us the testimony of the good Mr. Andrews that each woman has to serve three males. These three are indentured labourers; there may be others occasionally. We have translated Mr. Andrews' language, but the readers will easily guess the meaning of the word "serve."

If the system is abolished, our helpless sisters will be saved from dishonour or, at any rate, we shall be free of the responsibilty. It is plainly our duty to see this done. So long as we are ignorant of the snake under our bed we can sleep in peace, but only till then. The moment we become aware of the presence of the venomous companion, we get alarmed; we should react in similar fashion to indenture in Fiji. So long as we were ignorant of the horrible conditions of our sisters living in Fiji, we could rest and sleep in peace. But now? It is a sin to keep quiet even for a moment.

When the whole of India understands this, the immorality in Fiji will not go on for an hour longer. There are lawyers who ask how we can end lawful contracts of indenture, how we can put pressure on the Fiji whites. There can only be one answer to this. A law contrary to morality, a law which upholds immorality, is no law. To respect such a law is to be a partner to immorality. How did it ever happen that a law which served as an instrument of immorality continued to this day? This is the pertinent question.

We hope an appeal will reach the government immediately from every village and town of Gujarat, demanding that the system of indenture in Fiji be abolished forthwith. Mr. Andrews has fixed December 31 as the final date of its abolition. He does not have the power of a government in his hands; but he has greater power than that: the solemn voice of his grief-stricken soul. We wish every man and every woman hears this voice and does his or her duty.

¤　¤　¤

*Twenty years after abolition was achieved, Andrews reflected on the meaning of that struggle in a meditation delivered to members of a Christian ashram. He wanted his listeners to understand the connection between political involvement and the service of Christ. After telling the story of the campaign, he poses a question.*

¤   ¤   ¤

What should this mean to us, as Christians? Surely it completely destroys the idea, which is in some people's minds even today, that Christianity is a purely spiritual religion, having nothing whatever to do with political affairs. Here was a definitely political issue. Yet, how could anyone who has heard the voice of Jesus saying, "I was sick, I was in prison," refuse to answer His call? For "in their afflictions, He was afflicted." In every one of those poor and distressed Indians, bound down to servile labour in the plantations, under these immoral conditions, He, the Son of Man, was suffering. It was all "done unto Him."

Thus it was Jesus who appealed to us, by the constraining power of His love, to bring all this evil to an end. His love that made those who took up the cause of abolition determine never to lay it down till the whole system was ended. Thank God! This was accomplished at last on January 1st, 1920.

Let me now show you what a change has taken place, since indenture was abolished. In the year 1936, I went back to Fiji after an absence of nearly twenty years, and fifteen years after the abolition of the evil. The difference that I saw there was amazing! It was as if some great weight had been lifted, and people were breathing again. The evil system had been wiped out, including all its immoral effects. Men and women were begining eagerly to build up their homes again, with new freedom and joy. No sight could be a happier one than that of the little children, clean and tidy, going to school, with bright faces, instead of the miserable and dirty children in what used to be called the coolie lines.

While, therefore, it is a fact that *every* permanent remedy for social *evils must* begin from within, and have its motive power in the heart; and while it is certain, in this sense, that Christ's words are eternally true when He says,"The Kingdom of God is *within* you," yet at the same time it may be possible, by removing some disease from the body politic, to give free play for these inner forces so that they regain control, and drive out the rest of the evil from the body. Such a cancerous growth was slavery, a century ago; and such was the Indian indentured labour system, which supplied the British colonies with Indian labour, under immoral conditions, in our own age.

¤   ¤   ¤

*Andrews moved easily from politics to religion to poetry. He captured his motivating vision in this poem written at Simla in July, 1915, a poem entitled "The Indentured Coolie."*

There he crouched,
Back and arms scarred, like a hunted thing
Terror-stricken.
All within me surged towards him,
While the tears rushed.
Then, a change.
Through his eyes I saw Thy glorious face—
Ah, the wonder!
Calm, unveiled in deathless beauty,
Lord of sorrow.

# Chapter 4

## Amritsar

When Gandhi returned to India for good in the summer of 1914, he came as a celebrity because of the success of his work in South Africa. It was at that time that Tagore bestowed on him the title of "Mahatma," or "Great Soul."

It is important to note that in these years Gandhi still considered himself a loyal British subject; he had not yet decided that there was no viable alternative to the departure of the British. As he began to assume political leadership in Congress after 1916, Gandhi's concerns increasingly lay with what he called "the moral regeneration of India"—the evil, he insisted, lay not in British rule but in modern civilization. India must unlearn the lessons of the West and reconstruct the traditional culture of her villages and peasants. Gandhi was convinced that India's welfare lay in a revival of the village and its traditions of craftsmanship, particularly those of spinning and weaving. His spinning wheel became the central symbol of regeneration.

*Gandhi still thought that the British Empire existed "for the welfare of the world," and for this he was criticized by Indian nationalists. Gandhi even thought that if Indians were to assert their rights as British subjects, it was their duty to defend the British Empire in time of war. It was this same conviction that led him to offer to raise troops for the British army in the First World War and led to a serious dispute with Andrews.*

*Here Andrews gives us the background to this dispute.*

¤     ¤     ¤

[In 1914] Gandhi returned to India by way of England and arrived at Southampton on the very night of the outbreak of the war. With characteristic promptness and self-sacrifice he offered the next morning his services at the India Office as stretcherbearer and hospital worker. He promised to serve in any capacity as a minister to the sick and wounded for the duration of the war. His services were accepted and he worked unremittingly; but an attack of pleurisy in England in November 1914, which was nearly fatal, made it imperative for him to return to the warmer climate of India. When he had fully recovered, he twice volunteered for hospital work in Mesopotamia. He was prepared to raise a company of 500 workers who should be under the strictest discipline and ready for devoted service. But on both occasions his offer failed to obtain acceptance at the headquarters of the British Government in India.

His last act of service on behalf of the Allied cause, in whose righteousness at that time he fully believed, was to start a recruiting campaign in his own province of Gujarat to enlist Indian fighting men. This was, and has always been, to me quite inexplicable on his part, because he himself is the strictest believer in moral force as contrasted with physical force. I have mentioned this inconsistency because it pained me very greatly at the time and led directly in his own case to another almost fatal illness and complete physical prostration. During this critical time of illness I was with him and learned to know the beauty of his character as I had never known it before.

◘    ◘    ◘

*An exchange of letters in 1918 reveals the serious disagreement between the two friends. The letters from Gandhi to Andrews, which follow, require close reading. One senses, as Andrews did, that the logic is flawed; yet some of Gandhi's deepest concerns of that period in his development are expressed here. First, Gandhi was convinced that* ahimsa, *or non-violence, must not spring from cowardice.* Ahimsa *is for the brave, even if that bravery must first be learned in war. Second, India's future must not be a repeat of its past in showing any lack of resolve against its foes. Third, loyalty to the British Empire must be maintained.*

◘    ◘    ◘

As for my offer you know that . . . . I have said I should kill neither friend nor foe. Regarding those who want to fight but will not, either out of cowardice or spite against the British, what is my duty? Must I not say, "If you can follow my path, so much the better, but if you cannot, you ought to give up cowardice or spite and fight." You cannot teach *ahimsa* to a man who cannot kill. You cannot make a dumb man appreciate the beauty and merit of silence. Although I know that silence is most excellent, I do not hesitate to take means that would enable the dumb man to regain his speech.

I do not believe in any government, but parliamentary government is perhaps better than capricious rule. I think it will be clear to you that I shall best spread the gospel of *ahimsa*, or *satyagraha*, by asking the *himsak* [military men] to work out their *himsa* in the least offensive manner, and may succeed, in the very act, in making them realize the better worth of *ahimsa*. If I have not made the position clear, you should try if you can to come down.

¤　　¤　　¤

*In his reply, Andrews said he did not see the analogy of the dumb man: "It seems dangerously near the argument that the Indian who has forgotten altogether the bloodlust might be encouraged to learn it again first and then repudiate it afterwards of his own account." He agreed that it would be a free India, not a subjected India, that would give the world the highest example of* ahimsa, *but also asked: "Cannot you conceive of that very freedom being won by moral force only, not by the creation of a standing army to meet the army of occupation?"*

*Andrews went on to assert that there had been a past renunciation of "bloodlust" on the part of the Indian people, and that they were somehow instinctively ready to make that renunciation. Here he was on weak ground, as Gandhi was quick to point out.*

¤　　¤　　¤

July 6, 1918

My Dear Charlie,

I have your letters. I prize them. They give me only partial consolation. My difficulties are deeper than you have put them. All you raise I can answer. I must attempt in this letter to reduce my own to writing. They just now possess me to the exclusion of everything else. All the other things I seem to be doing purely mechanically. This hard thinking has told upon my physical system. I hardly want to talk to anybody. I do not want even to write anything, not even these thoughts of mine. I am therefore falling back upon dictation to see whether I can clearly express them. I have not yet reached the bottom of my difficulties, much less have I solved them. The solution is not likely to affect my immediate work. But of the failure I can now say nothing. If my life is spared I must reach the secret somehow.

You say: "Indians as a race did repudiate it, bloodlust, with full consciousness in days gone by and deliberately took their choice to stand on the side of humanity."

Is this historically true? I see no sign of it either in the Mahabharata or the Ramayana. I am not now thinking of these works in their spiritual meanings. The incarnations are described as certainly bloodthirsty, revengeful and merciless to the enemy. They have been credited with having resorted to tricks also for the sake of overcoming the enemy. The battles are described with no less zest than now, and the warriors are equipped with weapons of destruction such as could be possibly conceived by the human imagination. The finest hymn composed by Tulsidas in praise of Rama gives the first place to his ability to strike down the enemy.

Then take the Mahomedan period. The Hindus were not less eager than the Mahomedans to fight. They were simply disorganized, physically weakened, and torn by internal dissensions. The code of Manu prescribes no such renunciation that you impute to the race. Buddhism, conceived as a doctrine of universal forbearance, signally failed, and, if the legends are true, the great Shankaracharya did not hesitate to use unspeakable cruelty in banishing Buddhism out of India. And he succeeded!

Then the English period. There has been compulsory renunciation of arms, but not the desire to kill. Even among the Jains the doctrine has signally failed. They have a superstitious horror of bloodshed, but they have as little regard for the life of the enemy as a European. What I mean to say is that they would rejoice equally with anybody on earth over the destruction of the enemy. All then that can be said of India is that individuals have made serious attempts, with greater success than elsewhere, to popularize the doctrine. But there is no warrant for the belief that it has taken deep root among the people.

You say further: "My point is that it has become an unconscious instinct, which can be awakened any time as you yourself have shown." I wish it was true. But I see that I have shown nothing of the kind. When friends told me here that passive resistance was taken up by the people as a weapon of the weak, I laughed at the libel, as I called it then. But they were right and I was wrong. With me alone, and a few other co-workers, it came out of our strength and was described as *satyagraha*, but with the majority it was purely and simply passive resistance that they resorted to, because they were too weak to undertake methods of violence. This discovery was forced on me repeatedly in Kaira. The people here, being comparatively freer, talked to me without reserve, and told me plainly that they took up my remedy because they were not strong enough to take up the other, which they undoubtedly held to be far more manly than mine.

I fear that the people, whether in Champaran or in Kaira, would not fearlessly walk to the gallows, or stand a shower of bullets and yet say, in one case, "We will not pay the revenue" and in the other, "We will not work for you." They have it not in them. And I contend that they will not regain the fearless spirit until they have received the training to defend themselves. *Ahimsa* was preached to man when he was in full vigour of life and able to look his adversaries straight in the face. It seems to me that full development of body-force is a *sine qua non* of full appreciation and assimilation of *ahimsa*.

I do agree with you that India with her moral force could hold back from her shores any combination of armies from the West or the East or North or the South. The question is, how can she cultivate this moral force? Will she have to be strong in body before she can understand even the first principles of this moral force? It will not come until there is an atmosphere of freedom and fearlessness on the soil. How to produce that atmosphere? Not without the majority of the inhabitants feeling that they are well able to protect themselves from the violence of man or beast. Now I think I can state my difficulty. It is clear that before I can give a child an idea of *moksha* [liberation from the body] I must let it grow into full manhood. I must allow it to a certain extent to be even attached to the body, and then when it has understood the body and so the world around it, may I easily demonstrate the transitory nature of the body and the world, and make it feel that the body is given not for the indulgence of self, but for its liberation.

Even so must I wait for instilling into any mind the doctrine of *ahimsa*, i.e., perfect love, when it has grown to maturity by having its full play through a vigorous body. My difficulty now arises in the practical application of the idea. What is the meaning of having a vigorous body? Must every individual go through the practice or is it enough that a free atmosphere is created and the people will, without having to bear arms, etc., imbibe the necessary personal courage from their surroundings? I believe that the last is the correct view, and, therefore, I am absolutely right as things are in calling upon every Indian to join the army, always telling him at the same time that he is doing so not for the lust of blood, but for the sake of learning not to fear death.

. . . . There is not a single recruiting speech in which I have not laid the greatest stress upon this part of a warrior's duty. There is no speech in which I have yet said, "Let us go to kill the Germans." My refrain is, "Let us go and die for the sake of India and the Empire." I feel that, supposing that the response to my call is overwhelming and we all go to France and turn the scales against the Germans, India will then have a claim to be heard and she may then dictate a peace that will last. Suppose further that I have succeeded in raising an army of fearless men, they fill the trenches and with hearts of love lay down their guns and challenge the Germans to shoot them—their fellow men—I say that even the German heart will melt. I refuse to credit it with exclusive fiendishness. So it comes to this, that under exceptional circumstances, war may have to be resorted to as a necessary evil, even as the body is. If the motive is right, it may be turned to the profit of mankind and that an *ahimsa*-ist may not stand aside and look on with indifference but must make his choice and actively co-operate or actively resist.

Your fear about my being engrossed in the political strife and intrigues may be entirely set aside. I have no stomach for them, least at the present moment, had none even in South Africa. I was in the political life because therethrough lay my own liberation. Montagu said, "I am surprised to find you taking part in the political life of the country!" Without a moment's thought I replied, "I am in it because without it I cannot do my religious and social work," and I think the reply will stand good to the end of my life.

You can't complain of my having given you only a scrap of a letter. Instead of a letter, I have inflicted upon you what may almost read like an essay. But it was necessary that you should know what is passing in my mind at the present moment. You may now pronounce your judgement and mercilessly tear my ideas to pieces where you find them to be wrong.

I hope you are getting better and stronger. I need hardly say that we shall all welcome you when you are quite able to undertake the journey.

With love,
Mohan

¤   ¤   ¤

*The following letter, more peremptory in tone, makes clear that Gandhi is answering not only Andrews but Tagore, with whom Andrews had been traveling in China and Japan. Tagore had spoken in Japan and had been greeted by derision from a Japanese audience when he warned against Japan's imitating the militaristic spirit and behavior of the West. The battle of Plassey in 1757, to which Gandhi refers, was a military defeat for Indian forces which paved the way for British domination.*

¤   ¤   ¤

July 29, 1918

My Dear Charlie,

I must indulge myself again. I begin to perceive a deep meaning behind the Japanese reluctance to listen to the message of a prophet from a defeated nation. War will be always with us. There seems to be no possibilty of the whole human nature becoming transformed. *Moksha* and *ahimsa* are for individuals to attain. Full practice of *ahimsa* is inconsistent with possession of wealth, land, or rearing of children. There is real *ahimsa* in defending my wife and children even at the risk of striking down the wrongdoer. It is perfect *ahimsa* not to strike him but intervene to receive his blows. India did neither on the field of Plassey. We were a cowardly mob warring against one another, hungering for the East India Company's silver and selling our souls for a mess of pottage.

And so have we remained more or less—more rather than less—up to today. There was no *ahimsa* in their miserable performance, notwithstanding examples of personal bravery and later corrections of the exaggerating accounts of those days. Yes, the Japanese reluctance was right. I do not know sufficiently what the fathers of old did. They suffered, I expect, not out of their weakness, but out of their strength. I find great difficulties in recruiting, but do you know that not one man has yet objected because he would not kill? They object because they fear to die. This unnatural fear of death is ruining the nation. For the moment, I am simply thinking of the Hindus. Total disregard of death in a Mahomedan lad is a wonderful possession.

I have not written a coherent letter today but I have given you indications of my mental struggle.

With deep love,<br>
Yours,<br>
Mohan

¤     ¤     ¤

*In a letter to a close mutual friend, an Indian Christian, Gandhi refers to his disagreement with Andrews and puts an interesting interpretation on the non-violence of Jesus. The friend was Susil Rudra, principal of St. Stephen's College in Delhi. His happiness, to which Gandhi refers in his letter, lay in the fact that one of his sons had just been appointed a second lieutenant. Obviously Gandhi did not have to convince him on the main point at issue.*

¤     ¤     ¤

July 29, 1918

Dear Mr. Rudra,

I thank you for letting me share your happiness. Sudhir is a brick. Yes he is doing good work, and so are the other boys each in his own line. It is the result of orderly training.

While you approve of my recruiting campaign, Charlie is fighting it out with me. He thinks it is just likely that I am deluding myself. He thinks that this activity of mine may injure my service to the cause of *ahimsa*. I have taken it up to serve that very cause. I know that my responsibilty is great. It was equally great when I was supine, feeling that recruiting was not my line. There was a danger of those who put faith in my word becoming or remaining utterly unmanly, falsely believing that it was *ahimsa*. We must have the ability in the fullest measure to strike and then perceive the inabilty of brute force and renounce the power. Jesus had the power to consume his enemies to ashes but he refrained and permitted himself to be killed, for he so loved, etc.

Yours sincerely,
M.K.G.

¤　¤　¤

*It was Andrews who would have the last word on the subject, in a letter to Gandhi dated February 2, 1920. He actually gives the last word to Tagore and then accepts a measure of blame for himself, acknowledging the need to do* prayaschitta *(penance) along with his friend, since they had both participated in a war conference convened by the Viceroy, Lord Chelmsford, in May of 1918. Gandhi moved the resolution endorsing the war effort at the conference, while Andrews had played a smaller role, lending consent and support only by his presence.*

*Gandhi's illness, to which Andrews refers, seems to have been owing to some combination of dysentery and nervous breakdown. Through the whole painful business he had worn himself out and won only a few recruits for the British war effort.*

¤   ¤   ¤

I had a letter from Gurudev [Tagore], two days ago. It had in it this terrible passage, which I had to acknowledge was partly, if not wholly, true. He wrote, "Not very long ago we said to our rulers, 'We are willing to sacrifice our principle and persuade our men to join in a battle about whose merit they had not the least notion, only in exchange, we shall claim your favour at the end of it.' It was beautifully weak, it was sinful. And now we must acknowledge our responsibilty to the extent of our late effort at recruiting—for turning our men into a mercenary horde drenching the soil of Asia with brother's blood for the sake of self-aggrandisement of a people wallowing in the mire of imperialism."

That sentence hits me very hard indeed . . . . because I did not stop you, but rather encouraged you at Delhi in May 1918, at that War Conference, when neither of us stood firm but allowed the Viceroy to twist us around the little finger. I have always felt that I had to do *prayaschitta* for that, and that your illness was in a great measure your own prayaschitta which was sent to you—I know we were blind, but our blindness was almost willful blindness.

¤   ¤   ¤

*This exchange of letters between Andrews and Gandhi is particularly striking when we see how dramatically Gandhi's attitude to British rule and the beneficence of colonial policy was to change only a year later. Up to this point Gandhi's campaigns of* satyagraha *had been for strictly limited objectives and successfully and peacefully waged, but the press of events soon demanded a wider field. The* catalyst was the growing British anxiety about terrorism and dissension, which issued in the Rowlatt Bill of March, 1919, ordering heavy penalties and a secret trial for anyone suspected of terrorist activity. Gandhi began to tour the country preaching a nation-wide satyagraha campaign against the bill—his first real entry into active Indian politics.

The campaign consisted of protest processions, hartals, or work stoppages, and acts of civil disobedience. The Viceroy was warned of all this beforehand. Response to Gandhi's call was huge—millions responded—and it was the first real mass movement of the Indian people toward liberation. These hartals took place in all the major cities.

The campaign was intended to be non-violent but violence flared up on both sides, especially in the Punjab. This province in India's northwest had suffered the loss of many of its men and boys during the war. Anti-colonialist feeling was running high, and the actions against the Rowlatt Bill brought them to fever pitch.

On April 10, 1919, riots broke out in the city of Amritsar, where mobs burned and looted buildings, including churches. Several Europeans were killed. On April 13th a bloody reprisal by the British took place.

Twenty thousand people had assembled on that date in an illegal meeting held in an enclosed square called Jallianwala Bagh, when, without warning, a military detachment opened fire upon them with machine guns. Hundreds were killed; over a thousand were wounded. Gandhi called off the satyagraha on April 18, after a penitential fast of three days.

In the immediate aftermath of the massacre, Gandhi persuaded Andrews to travel to the Punjab on a fact-finding mission. He was to determine what had happened at Jallianwala Bagh and what was going on under the martial law that since had been imposed in the region. The British government was organizing its own committee of inquiry under Lord Hunter, but Gandhi knew that Andrews—better than any governmental committee—would be able to elicit the truth from a terrorized people.

It was another job of fact-finding for Andrews, and he approached it in his systematic way, wanting to compile information that would be of value both to the government and to the Indian people. It was also an act of penance by one Englishman on behalf of his many countrymen, who had allowed such a terrible wrong to occur but who failed to see the evil they had done. The greatest symbol of that failure would be the action of the House of Lords when it cleared the name of General Dyer, who had given the order to fire on the people. They justified his action as having been necessary to save British rule in India.

Andrews' mission of reconciliation is brought into sharpest focus for us when we read about his encounter with a Sikh village headman who had suffered at the hands of the British. Andrews described the incident years later in his book Christ in the Silence. Writing there about the new commandment in John's gospel, that we should love one another, he recalled this meeting in the Punjab and used it to illustrate the story of Christ stooping down to wash the disciples' feet.

¤   ¤   ¤

Among the crudely brutal acts which are always likely to occur under martial law, a grievous injustice had been done in India some years ago. A young Sikh village headman, with a fine record of service as a soldier, both on the North West Frontier of India and also in France, had been hurriedly taken out at break of day and flogged in the presence of his fellow-villagers on the suspicion of having cut the telegraph wires some two miles away from his village.

Positive proof was offered me that this extremely hasty punishment, meted out instantly under martial law, was quite unjustified, and that he had been innocent of any offence. It was quite impossible at the time, in the stress of circumstance, to get justice immediately done, and I could see that it was the moral wound which had cut deepest of all, far deeper than any subsequent act of reparation could assuage. Already he had shown clear signs of insanity, through brooding over his intolerable wrong till it had clouded all his mind. His friends had begun to be afraid even to go near him lest some mad act of violence might happen. All day and night he stayed in one room overlooking the gateway of the town, and refused to leave it. His friends had come to me asking my help in their distress.

On drawing near to him my whole heart went out in pity for him. But he shunned me at first, even while I spoke to him the tenderest words of sympathy and love. Then suddenly, prompted from within by a subconscious memory of Christ's act, I stooped down and touched his feet, asking from him at the same time pardon for the great wrong my fellow-countrymen had committed.

When he saw what I had done, he drew his feet very quickly away, almost with a shock; then he burst into tears. For a long time we remained together, while he cried his heart out with convulsive sobs which seemed as though they would never cease. When at last, with deep emotion, I asked him if the past had all been forgotten and forgiven, he answered "Yes," and his face was lighted up with a new joy and peace. His spirit had found its release and his heart had become again as the heart of a little child.

This illustration, which I have tried to tell quite simply as it all happened, may serve to make plain in human ways some of the first steps in the marvellous working of the divine love. For it was truly the constraining love of Christ that carried me forward. His, too, was the divine power to heal and to bless. A thousand, thousand times Christ's own love had forgiven me, a sinner; He had thus made me to understand what forgiveness meant to the spirit of a fellow-man.

¤   ¤   ¤

*When his investigation had been completed, Andrews bid farewell to the Punjab in a speech delivered at a mass meeting in Lahore on November 15, 1919.*

*In these remarks, Andrews summarized the conclusions of his inquiry and issued a call for reconciliation. The "probing of the wounds" refers to the work of Lord Hunter's committee, while "matters of immediate practical urgency" concern his successful efforts to free a Punjabi patriot sentenced by the military authorities to life imprisonment. Andrews' most important allusion is to the death of Miss Sherwood, headmistress of a girls' school in Amritsar who was brutally set upon by a mob on April 10th. After the massacre General Dyer ordered that anyone walking down the street where she had been attacked must go on all fours, the famous "crawling order" that Gandhi resented as much as the massacre itself.*

¤   ¤   ¤

It is a very difficult thing to say goodbye after months of such close and intimate fellowship in work, as we have had together both in Delhi and in the Punjab. My words will therefore be few. Except for matters of immediate practical urgency, I have kept my lips sealed on all controversial points both on the platform and in the press during the time I have been personally working. But now that I am leaving immediately for South Africa and shall not be returning for at least four months, I don't think it would be honest on my part to go away silently without any statement at all of what I have seen and witnessed. I wish to go at once to the main issues and I think I can put my own position quite briefly in the following manner: I hold as strongly as possible after my inquiry that no provocation whatever can excuse the cowardly and brutal murders of Englishmen by the mob which occurred at Amritsar and elsewhere, nor the burning of the holy places of the Christian religion. Most cowardly and dastardly of all I regard the murderous attack on Miss Sherwood, who was loved by every Indian who knew her and who was a true follower and disciple of the gentle Saviour Christ. But just as I condemn, without one single word of palliation or excuse, these acts, so all the more utterly and entirely do I condemn the cold and calculated massacre at Jallianwala Bagh.

The massacre of Glencoe in English history is no greater a blot on the fair name of my country than the massacre at Amritsar. I am not speaking from idle rumour. I have gone into every single detail with all the care and thoroughness that a personal investigation could command and it remains to me an unspeakable disgrace, indefensible, unpardonable, inexcusable. And I am obliged to go on from that incident to what followed under martial law. I have seen with my own eyes the very men who have endured the crawling order, the compulsion to grovel on their bellies in the dust, the public flogging which was administered to hundreds of men and a hundred other desecrations of man's image, which according to our Christian scriptures is made in the likeness of God.

This ruthless and deliberate emasculation of manhood by the brute force of the military and the police appears to me no less an indelible stain on the fair honour of my country than the massacre at Jallianwala Bagh itself. These are the very few words which I have felt compelled as an Englishman to say with regard to the culminating acts of the Disturbance. Every day that I have been working side by side with my Indian fellow-workers, the deep sense of the wrong done has come home to me, and each act has been in very truth an act of penance, of atonement, an act of reparation for my country.

When in Lahore, I have gone out each morning to watch the sun rise over the great and noble eucalyptus trees in the Montgomery gardens and have walked there all alone trying to collect my thoughts for the day's work. And this morning there came to me out of the stormy time I have been passing through these words from my own scriptures:

> He maketh His sun to rise upon the just and upon
> the unjust. Be ye therefore perfect even as your
> Father in heaven is perfect.

These were the very words of Christ, my Master, which taught his disciples that forgiveness was the final thing in life, not vengeance, love was the end, not hate.

That same word was uttered long ago in India itself by Buddha who came to save and help mankind. It was this and this alone which was given to me on this last day in Lahore before my voyage out.

We must probe down to the depth the wounds that have been made in order to draw out all the evil from them. But the last is not probing but binding up the wounds—the work of healing.

And I would urge you as you go forward and face all the facts of evil which have been done, not to dwell merely upon vengeance but rather upon forgiveness, not linger in the dark night of hate but to come out into the glorious sunshine of God's love.

¤    ¤    ¤

*Gandhi had not read this speech of Andrews' in advance, but we can see from his own introduction of Andrews at that same meeting how closely their thoughts matched.*

*Gandhi, too, describes Andrews' actions as penance under-
taken for the wrongdoing of his people.*

*While Andrews appealed to the authority of Jesus in the
Sermon on the Mount, Gandhi refers to a bit of Hindu
mythology to illustrate the nature of love's response to
brutality. He tells his listeners that they are to love the
English not in a blind way, but rather in the way that the
legendary Prahlad loved his father. The tale of Prahlad
would have been known to the members of his audience
from their childhood. He was the son of a cruel and
tyrannical king who did not believe in God. Himself a
believer, Prahlad was tormented by his father on account
of his faith. Once the ruler even had the son thrown into
the fire, but he was miraculously rescued. In the final
episode of the tale, the god Narasinha (half human, half
lion) puts the king to death for mocking his son's belief.
Prahlad is then installed as king in his father's stead.*

*An Indian acquaintance who told me the story assured
me that Prahlad loved his father through his ordeal. So
Gandhi's choice of this tale allowed him to teach love
without denying the cruelty of a regime that had to be
brought to an end.*

¤    ¤    ¤

Mr. Andrews is like a brother to me. I therefore find it difficult
to say anything about him. The sacred relationship between
us stands in the way. I can, however, say this, that Mr.
Andrews is a staunch Englishman but has dedicated his life to
India. Through his actions he tells us: "Even if you feel that
you are oppressed by my countrymen, do not think ill of them,
look at me." If we revere Mr. Andrews, it behoves us to imitate
his love. Our love must not be blind, but such as Prahlad
showed for his father. Mr. Andrews' life teaches us that,

although we must resent and resist oppression and injustice, it is also our duty to bear no enmity towards the wrongdoer.

The Government has placed us in a difficult position. They have refused even a temporary release of the prisoners. We had intended to give evidence before Lord Hunter's committee, but the Government has made this impossible.

We must not, however, yield to anger on account of this thoughtless step of the Government's. Mr. Andrews has done far more for India than many Indians have done. He has not spared his countrymen, but that does not mean that his love for the English is any the less. In like manner, we, too, can fight for justice and self-respect without harbouring ill will against the British or the Government.

Mr. Andrews has poured out his very life for India. He is no ordinary Englishman. He is a man of great learning, comes of an illustrious family, is a poet and a theologian. If he had wished, he could have become a high dignitary, he could have been the principal of a big college or, if he had wanted, he could have been in a high position as a priest. But he has not cared for wealth or for position and, today, wanting nothing for himself, he is ever on his feet in the service of India. What is our duty towards such an Englishman? As long as there is even one Andrews among the British people, we must, for the sake of such as one, bear no hatred to them. If we hate them, we cannot bear real love for Mr. Andrews and we shall forfeit the right to accept his service. This is clear enough.

The question is: When massacres like the one at Jallianwala Bagh take place, when British soldiers abuse us, kick us, debar us from sitting with them in trains, British officers want to keep all power to themselves and British merchants try to monopolize the principal trade of India, how can we help being angry with them? How can we ever feel affection for them? The difficulty is obvious. Wherever one turns, one finds hatred, anger, scorn and falsehood. When Indians do not always feel affection for one another, what can we expect from them with regard to the British? But these doubts arise from want of faith in God. An intellectual acceptance of the existence of God does not make one a believer. To believe in God but not love people is a contradiction in terms. Faith implies truth and love. If these qualities could shine forth within us in their perfection, we would ourselves be God.

Accepting this truth, we should move in its direction. This is the lesson to be learnt from Mr. Andrews' life: his penance is for this, it is the true meaning of his *tapascharya* [ascetic self-denial] hidden from the eyes of men. I have seen him sitting silent for hours in our homes. Even when we have disregarded him, I have seen that he has shown no anger. I have seen him eating contentedly whatever was offered him in our homes. I have known him setting out for South Africa at a moment's notice at the late Mr. Gokhale's behest. This is true and silent *tapascharya*. His work on our behalf in South Africa and other countries is there for us all to see and, therefore, we recognize it as such. But the invisible sacrifices that he is ever making are even more precious.

But it is not only out of respect for Mr. Andrews that we must banish all hatred for the British. By doing so we shall ensure early success of our efforts, for if we work on in patience, as he does with perseverance and with all regard for truth, the British will have no occasion to visit their evil propensities on us. And just as he is able to do the work of many, standing alone, so also if even one Indian follows in his footsteps, he will do as much alone, and will accelerate our progress.

¤    ¤    ¤

*Each man appealed to the authority of different religious traditions in India to make the point that was of central importance to them both, that hatred and vengeance were*

to be overcome by love. In addition to Christ, Andrews
mentions the Buddha in his address. This was no casual
reference, because as we read in his book, The Sermon on
the Mount, he gave credit to Gautama the Buddha as the
one who first discovered "the law of love."

¤    ¤    ¤

We have to go a very long way in human history if we would
trace right back the silent growth of this idea of returning good
for evil. In the life of Gautama the Buddha it formed the
supreme discovery which he made when he sought to break
the chain of suffering wherewith human life had hitherto
appeared to be inextricably bound. The wheel of that suffering,
so it seemed to him as he meditated upon our common human
destiny, only revolved the faster at each new act of retaliation.
But if the opposite of retaliation was accomplished, and good
was returned instead of evil, the wheel of suffering, at that
point at least, began to revolve more slowly.

¤    ¤    ¤

Andrews found the same teaching in the Sikh religion.
In his book Sadhu Sundar Singh, the story of a Christian
mystic who had been brought up in the Sikh tradition, he
records that some of his own happiest days in India had
been spent with the Sikhs, "dwelling with them in their own
homes, listening to their devotional songs, and sharing
their life in common with them. I can say with conviction
that the sacred words of their Gurus, repeated by their lips,
have sunk deeply into their hearts. It would be difficult to
find more generous or forgiving people."

Their sacred words sank into Andrews' heart as well. He
especially valued the following text from the Sikh scriptures
(the Granth Saheb), a text which reminded him of the
Sermon on the Mount.

Farid, if a man beat thee, strike him not
but stoop and kiss his feet.
Farid, if thy soul hath longing for the Lord,
become as grass for men to tread on.
Farid, when one man breaketh thee, and another
trampleth on thee, then thou enterest truly
the Temple of God.

*In another telling of his healing encounter with the Sikh village headman, we learn that Andrews appealed directly to this tradition when he spoke with him. Before bowing down to touch his feet, he said: "Guru Nanak, in the Granth Saheb, enjoins on us forgiveness. I want you to forgive me. The sin is mine because it is my countryman's."*

*In Gandhi's thought, at its very best, we also find this ability to see one central truth reflected by different people in different religious traditions. This is expressed with great clarity in a brief essay entitled "We are All One," which appeared in* Navajivan *in 1930. These reflections by Gabdhi should help to deepen our understanding of the penance undertaken by Andrews, whom he here calls Deenabandhu, or "brother of the humble."*

¤　¤　¤

God is present in all of us. For my part, every moment I experience the truth that though many, we are all one. He does not reveal Himself in the same form in all of us, or rather the hearts of all of us not being alike, we do not see Him in the same form—just as in mirrors of different colors and shapes a thing is reflected in different colors and shapes.

From this it follows that the sin of one is the sin of all. And hence it is not up to us to destroy the evildoer. We should, on the contrary, suffer for him. From this thought was born the idea of *satyagraha* and of civil disobedience of law. Criminal, violent, or uncivil disobedience is sin and ought to be abjured.

Non-violent disobedience can be a holy duty. It is with this thought that Deenabandhu Andrews has often said that he is doing atonement on behalf of the English.

# Chapter 5

## The Oppression of the Poor

*T*he man who had once so respected the British Empire that he recruited soldiers for its defense was now coming to the conclusion that the colonial system lacked any capacity for self-improvement. Britain had shown no sign of repentance for what had been done at Amritsar. Gandhi himself began to feel no longer a citizen, but a "pariah untouchable of the Empire."

The three years following Amritsar were years of intense political activity for both Andrews and Gandhi. Gandhi continued to dominate Congress while moving into new areas of dissent in order to widen the base of support for a movement towards self-rule for India. One of those areas concerned the demand that the British act to restore the suzerainty of the Sultan of Turkey as the Muslim Caliph. We will not attempt to explore this now-obscure question, only noting that Andrews disagreed with Gandhi in wanting the Arab countries to be free of renewed Turkish *dominance. On September 23rd, 1920, he wrote Gandhi in no uncertain terms about this question.*

¤    ¤    ¤

I hate the Khilafat doctrine of a Turkish Empire which was too sacred to be touched and which involved the refusal of independence to another race . . . . You have *not* made your meaning clear, and there is no trap in my question. It is as simple as A.B.C. Will you or will you not accept Arab and Armenian and Syrian independence in lands which are obviously theirs and not the Turks?

¤    ¤    ¤

*Gandhi bluntly refused to listen to his friend on this issue, which he was using to build his bridge to the Muslim community. He wrote to him: "I wish you would not concern yourself about my position on the Turkish question; i.e., you will depend upon it that I shall do nothing blindly." No welcoming of criticism there!*

*They disagreed as well on the central question of* swaraj *(independence). Congress itself was divided over the question of whether India should seek dominion status or instead should separate itself entirely from Britain. Andrews, for his part, wanted "independence, complete and perfect." It was his opposition to the "White Race idea," so prevalent among British people around the world, that led him to make his definition of* swaraj *so unequivocal. By contrast, Gandhi was at this time more of a gradualist. Of course he also held the responsibility of building as broad a base as possible within the Congress. In order to do that, he decided to propose to Congress that the Indian demand be for* swaraj *"either within or without the Empire." In urging this position in a resolution which the Congress*

*unanimously adopted in December, 1920, Gandhi referred*
*to Andrews' own stand.*

¤ ¤ ¤

There is room in this resolution for both: those who believe
that by retaining the British connection we can purify ourselves
and purify the British people, and those who have no such
belief. As, for instance, take the extreme case of Mr. Andrews.
He says all hope for India is gone for keeping the British
connection. He says there must be complete severance, complete independence. There is room enough in this creed for a
man like Mr. Andrews also.

¤ ¤ ¤

*While loosely defining the goal, a tight timetable was set*
*for achieving it. By the end of 1921 India was to be*
*self-governing. Gandhi launched a new satyagraha cam-*
*paign, calling upon Indians to boycott elections which had*
*been set for 1921 and to refuse to serve the colonial*
*government in any capacity. This non-cooperation move-*
*ment, spearheaded by the largely Hindu Congress, also*
*gained backing from the Muslim League. Students, lawyers*
*and many distinguished Indians from the professional clas-*
*ses lent support to this boycott of all institutions associated*
*with the British Raj. The boycott had only limited success,*
*but it raised the banner of* swaraj *and contributed to the*
*general atmosphere of insurrection brought on by continual*
*demonstrations and protests.*

*In the resolution presented to Congress, what Gandhi*
*sought was not just political independence but primarily*
*what he called national purification, or the moral regenera-*
*tion of India. His regenerative program was directed at*
*simplification and self-sufficiency in Indian life. He began*
*opening shops for the sale of handwoven* khaddar *cloth and*

*altered even his own simple Indian costume in order to wear only a loincloth—simple, austere, it identified him with the poorest of his people.*

*In this garb Gandhi began a new series of travels about India, visiting all the villages in turn—it marked the onset of his enormous popularity among the peasants. This strong presence among the peasants was what earned their loyalty, however, more than his programs. The loincloth, the spinning wheel, the homespun cloth—all pointed to Gandhi's superb instinct for powerful symbolic actions. These were the symbols of his crusade against India's central and overriding problem: the poverty of her peasantry.*

*In an editorial in* Young India *Andrews asked: "What is the sum and substance of the charge which Mahatma Gandhi laid against the British government in India? It may be summed up in a single phrase. He charged them with oppression of the poor."*

*Andrews was a ready follower in Gandhi's work for national regeneration. In a speech to students in Calcutta in January, 1921, he neatly presented the relationship between the external and internal dimensions of the movement for independence.*

¤   ¤   ¤

Independence, complete and perfect independence for India, is a religious principle with me because I am a Christian. But independence can never be won if the millions of the untouchables remain still in subjection. England cannot be England to me, the England I love, if she holds down Ireland and India by military force. And India cannot be India to you, the India of your dreams, and of my dreams too, if she does not give *swaraj* to her own depressed classes.

¤   ¤   ¤

*When Andrews taught Gandhi's program for national regeneration to Indian or English audiences, he liked to use the image of a hand, with its five fingers united by a single wrist, to state the five goals of the program and their one unifying principle.*

*Gandhi's five goals were the removal of untouchability, the prohibition of alcohol and drugs, the equality of man and woman, Hindu-Muslim unity, and the practice of swadeshi, the local provision of essential goods with special emphasis on the home-spinning of cloth. The unifying principle was ahimsa, without which Gandhi believed these goals could never be achieved in a spiritually healthy way.*

*This immense undertaking, involving conversion of hearts and societal change on so many levels, had to be presented in the simplest and most winning manner. Since the central issue for Andrews was the oppression of the poor, he loved to point to "the little poor man," Gandhi himself, as the living symbol of the movement. In these words from an article he wrote for the* Manchester Guardian *we can see how he does that. Andrews is writing during a visit to London sometime after the elections of 1921 and the imprisonment of Gandhi for his non-cooperation activities.*

¤   ¤   ¤

There has been no one in all my recollections of India who has understood the masses of the people like Mahatma Gandhi. He has held them in the hollow of his hand, and even from jail he still holds them to-day. The reasons for his great influence among the masses are two-fold—his saintliness and his voluntary poverty. He has lived their own life at all times and shared with them their desperate hardships. I have seen them coming to him and pleading, "Mahatmaji, do take more care of yourself. You are the only one in the world who understands us."

He is as different from any political leader in the West as it is possible to imagine. Only in a country so essentially religious as India would such a saint be made into a political leader. Perhaps the most wonderful thing of all, which shows his magnetic personality, is the fact that he has carried away with him on a wave of high enthusiasm very nearly the whole of the English-educated Indian community, men and women who have received the full training of the West.

In London I have been living in the Indian Students' Hostel, in Gower Street, and the reverence for Mahatma Gandhi's name is quite universal. There is no difference of opinion about him. This brings me to a second astonishing factor. The enthusiasm of Indian Mohammedans for him is as great as that of Hindus. He is the one man in modern times who has united the whole of India—rich and poor, caste and outcaste, Hindu and Muslim.

I have often pondered over the nature of his supreme influence, and more and more it has seemed to me to be due to the two things I have mentioned—his saintliness and his voluntary poverty. At one time, as every Indian knows, he was earning by his brilliant talents at the bar 5000 a year in Johannesburg, in South Africa. He kept open house with lavish hospitality.

But after reading Tolstoi's life and corresponding with him he abandoned everything he possessed and clad himself in the coarse homespun dress of a village peasant and began to plough and spin and weave at Tolstoi Farm. That was thirty years ago, and he has never since abandoned this life of extreme poverty.

When he goes to see the Viceroy he wears the same villager's dress. When he was asked at his trial, as a prisoner, to state his occupation, he said, "A farmer and a weaver." When he found that, owing to high prices after the war, it was impossible for the poverty-stricken villagers to wear more than a loin cloth, even in the cold weather, he determined to do the same.

The essential feature about Mahatma Gandhi's political programme was that he made the educated classes and the Government of India itself face the reality of the poverty of India. That poverty was to him the one vital problem to be solved. It was because he found the Government of India failing to face that problem that—to use his own word—he became a "rebel" and refused to cooperate with it.

¤    ¤    ¤

*In introducing his article, the editor of the* Guardian *identified Andrews as "perhaps the foremost living authority among white men on Indian opinion." The implicit racism of these phrases was typical of the time, but that was how his English admirers regarded him.*

*Andrews' detractors, meanwhile, were publicly calling for his arrest on charges of sedition. When asked by a reporter to respond to this accusation, which had been raised by a member of Parliament, Andrews simply referred to the government's need to hear the truth about the Indian people from someone like himself who had been living very closely with them. "If the Government of India cannot be told the truth about my experience among the masses without my being prosecuted for sedition, than we are in a very bad case indeed."*

*His work among the masses would take him across India into tense strike situations and other crises of the poor, and in such situations Andrews functioned as an agent of Gandhi. At times, merely by invoking Gandhi's name, he was able to win desperate people away from acts of violence. His own name, Deenabandhu Andrews, "brother of the humble," carried authority among the poor, who recognized in him the same saintliness and voluntary poverty that he ascribed to his teacher and friend.*

*A vivid picture of Andrews' work and of Gandhi's great influence in the early 1920s is provided in a small book he wrote entitled* The Oppression of the Poor. *The story told there concerns the desperate situation of some thousands of workers from the tea-gardens of Assam.*

*In 1921 a slump in the market for tea had resulted in idleness for many of these workers, who began leaving Assam for their homes in Calcutta in large numbers. The planters became alarmed by their leaving and intervened by denying them the free steamer passage they had expected to receive at the town of Chandpur. There they were stranded for a time as refugees in camps. In one very ugly incident, some of these camp dwellers were attacked and brutalized by Gurkha soldiers. In response to this, workers of the railway and steamship lines staged a protest strike; but in doing so, they cut off any means of egress from the town. When cholera set in, the plight of the people was truly dreadful.*

*Andrews promptly went to Chandpur in order to be with them. This account of his experience was written directly after the river steamers at last began taking the refugees away and he was able to return to Tagore's ashram to rest. The writing is passionate, but the writer—we are informed by those who worked alongside him—"was the very embodiment of peace and quietness, his very presence like balm in that excited and turbulent atmosphere." Gandhi was not himself present, yet we read that the hopes of the poor were all placed in him.*

¤   ¤   ¤

I have just come out of the furnace of affliction at Chandpur, where, in a cholera encampment, we were forced to see, day after day, the misery of our brothers and sisters and their little children, the refugees from Assam. If this record bears upon its surface the marks of the fire that burnt within us, I know that I shall be pardoned by all who read my words with understanding hearts. For I cannot, at such a time, keep a judicial aloofness from my subject. What we have just been through cannot be forgotten easily and lightly. I am giving hot memories, not cold, calculated thoughts, memories that still burn, even while I put them down in this Santiniketan ashram, where all around me are smiling with peace, in the pure joy of the fresh monsoon rains, and where nature herself is rejoicing in the beauty of new life.

The story has already been told, how the refugees came down from the tea gardens of Assam, emaciated beyond description; with stark hunger looking out of their eyes; with scarcely sufficient rags to cover their own nakedness; with little children who could hardly stand, their legs were so thin; with babies, pinched by hunger seeking in vain to draw nourishment from their mothers' breasts. I have seen many sights of misery and destitution before—in a sense, my life has been full of such sights. But I have never seen such utter misery as I saw among these refugees, when I met them on the railway platform at Naihati first of all, and then afterwards at Chandpur itself. What was the actual origin of their exodus, has still to be investigated. But one thing at least was evident, from the first to last, as we went in and out among them. In their destitution, they were miserable beyond description. Misery was the spur which goaded them forward on their journey. They had one hope left, to which they clung with a pathos that was as great as their suffering itself. It was the hope that, through Mahatma Gandhi, deliverance would come from all their burden of sorrow and affliction.

We watched each day these poor refugees from Assam in the cholera encampments on both sides of the river channel. We saw the courage that sustained them. We noticed how their spirits were kept up, during those long-drawn days of disappointment, by this hope which I have mentioned. To the men, who were refugees, it gave patience and endurance. To the women, it was like a passion of the soul; and they were able to enkindle something of their enthusiasm even in their little children. The national volunteers who worked among them used to talk to one another with wonder about this. It was a transforming faith that raised the whole scene above the commonplace, and touched it with spiritual beauty.

It is true, indeed, that Mahatma Gandhi himself has set his face firmly against any religious cult being originated in his name. He has repeatedly stated that he is an ordinary man with no claim to supernatural powers, beyond those to which ordinary men may attain by trust in the Supreme. But this devotion which we all witnessed at Chandpur, among those poor refugees, was rather the devotion to an idea than to a person. Mahatma Gandhi represented to them that idea, tinged with his own personality, and it filled their minds to the full. His name was the embodiment to them of their ultimate deliverance from oppression.

I must tell, at some length, one story which touched my heart most deeply. As we made our voyage with the last contingent of refugees from Chandpur to Goalundo, I had been walking to and fro along the decks of the crowded steamer. We had left behind us for good, oh! how thankfully, the cholera camp with all its misery. There was a busy eagerness among the refugees and a hum of expectation. One slender figure on the upper deck had stirred my compassion each time I had lingered near him. He was a little boy, about twelve years old, who had recovered (so I was told) from cholera, but was still so weak and thin, that he had to be carried on board and to lie on the deck during the voyage. While I stood beside him, we happened to pass out of the mid stream of the great river. The steamer came suddenly round a bend quite close to the shore. Bright, healthy children on the bank were running along and shouting,—"Gandhi Maharaj ki jai! Gandhi Maharaj ki jai!" [Victory to Gandhi!]

I looked at the invalid child on deck. His face shone with excitement and he raised his head with great difficulty. Then he waved his hand to the children running along the bank, and cried in a voice that was pitifully weak,—"Gandhi, Maharaj ki jai!"

Out of all the suffering and misery which we have been through, the haunting face of that child still stands out before my mind. There was something in it, through all the weakness, that seemed to have conquered death. It carried a light within the soul, which the Upanishad long ago named "the joy that is deathless."

The thought came like a flash to me, that here, in this child's faith, God himself was being revealed. Through all this suffering and pain, the words were finding their fulfilment—"God manifests himself in forms of deathless joy."

¤    ¤    ¤

*Both Andrews and Gandhi had a deep affection for children. When asked once by a friend how he could manage at Santiniketan ashram without the Holy, Andrews answered: "These children here, whom I am teaching, are my Holy Communion now."*

*A Hindu friend once told him that of all the sayings of Jesus, the one that spoke most clearly to him was his teaching that we must become as little children. "India," he said, "has always seen God in the innocence of the child."*

*His own vision of God in the face of a poor child led Andrews to reflect on the religious dimension of the non-cooperation movement of the masses.*

¤  ¤  ¤

In the midst of all these scenes, the question was borne in upon my mind with great insistence—"Is this that I have seen one of the signs of a new religious awakening throughout the length and breadth of India?" The poor of India, who have been so terribly oppressed by governments and priestcrafts, by landowners and profiteers, have cried to God for deliverance. They are becoming more and more certain that the hour of their freedom is at hand. During the past few months, it has been my own lot in life to travel over almost every part of the North of India, from East to West and from West to East—to places as far distant from one another as Sindh and East Bengal. On these journeys, I have seen strange happenings and witnessed a new spirit. This new spirit, I am convinced, goes far deeper than the political movement of our times. It has its own initial impulse from the poor.

Let me try to put my thought more concretely, even at the risk of repetition. The one thing that has impressed itself upon my heart and mind lately, more than any other, is this. The countless millions of the poor in India are all astir. They are coming forth out of their long dark night of ignorance and oppression. They have symbolized their yearning for deliverance in the person of Mahatma Gandhi. Pitifully, eagerly, pathetically, and sometimes almost tragically, they have placed their all—their destiny, their hopes, their aims, their very life itself—in his keeping. They are quite firm in their faith, that he alone can bring deliverance. This is not happening in one place only. Time after time, recently, I have been in the company of the poor and destitute and the outcaste, at gatherings where the untouchables and others have flocked together in crowds to meet me and I have listened with intense pain to the story of their afflictions. They appear now and everywhere to be taking their courage in both hands as they have never done before. The incidents with regard to oppression which they relate, with reference to forced labour and forced supplies and forced impositions by the police and subordinate officers, and also with reference to the forced impositions of caste customs and caste restrictions, equally tyrannical, have made my blood boil with indignation. They have often exhibited an emotion which was almost violent in its urge upwards towards the surface. I have seen in it something of that èlan vital, of which Henri Bergson writes, and have thanked God for it, even though it has not seldom startled me by its explosive energy. I do not think there can be any question, that a flame has been kindled within and the fire has begun to burn.

There is one picture, which may be given at this point, by way of illustration. I was at Patna Junction on my way back from Gorakhpur, where I had been enquiring concerning the home-coming of the refugees from Chandpur. Late in the day, as the sun was setting behind a ridge of dark monsoon clouds, with streaks of gold piercing through the gathering darkness, I was seated quietly on the platform trying to collect my thoughts while the evening was drawing to a close. Many persons had come to see me, and quiet was difficult at such a time or place. The porters and sweepers and others—whom the railway authorities call the "menial staff"—having heard of my arrival, gathered round me in a body. They knew that I was a friend of Mahatma Gandhi, and they welcomed me on that account.

At first, they greeted me in silence, with their uplifted hands placed together in an attitude of prayer. Then one of them, who was in the forefront as their leader, cried out, "Gandhi Maharaj ki jai!" It was not a conventional and jovial shout, such as is often heard from processions that pass along the street. It was rather the solemn call of religion. A light came into their eyes, and their hands continued to be uplifted in prayer to the end. It was like an act of evening worship.

After this, they went back to their various duties on the railway. It was only a momentary flash that I had seen, a look, a gaze, a gesture; but it spoke to me at once of the same emotion, which I had witnessed so many times before. It told me what depth of religious idealism there is in the hearts of the simple poor. That evening scene in Patna Junction, with the setting sun and the gathering darkness, brought back with a strange power the memory of sunsets at Chandpur. For there at Chandpur, again and again, just as the sun was setting, I had passed along the road and mingled with the groups of the Assam refugees, sitting in dejection, and had seen the look of hope return to their eyes, as they had raised the cry, "Gandhi Maharaj ki jai!"

¤　　¤　　¤

*Filled with the enthusiasm of this great movement of the poor across the land, Andrews tries to predict what its future will be. His greatest desire is that it should remain non-violent; his greatest fear is that it will not. Here we find him weighing the love of peace he knows to be within the people against the obduracy of the ruling class, both the English colonialists and the Indians who have identified with them.*

¤　　¤　　¤

I do not believe that the religious and social revolution in India, which is now so close upon us, will be violent in its character. There is an innate love of peace in India that is not present in any other country. It is not in vain that the teaching of the Buddha permeated India for more than a thousand years. But, while there may be no ultimate appeal to force and force alone, yet the misery of the conflict will be terrible indeed, if the present almost complete aloofness of the officials from the common people continues, and if these same officials set themselves in final opposition to those leaders whose lives are lived among the people and who suffer with the people.

The English education which the country has been receiving has created a gulf between the "classes" and the "masses," which is almost as wide as that between the Government and the poor. If the Bengal Government's recent action, when tried in the balance, has been found wanting, there has been much also that has been found wanting among those who have received to the full their English education, but, while obtaining it, have shamefully neglected the poor. The truth is, and it cannot be too clearly stated, the English mode of life, with its motor car comforts, continually prevents the educated Indian, just as much as it does the educated Englishman, from coming into close and intimate contact with the poor of India.

Mahatma Gandhi has written in *Young India* the following words: "The fact is that it is impossible for any Viceroy to see the truth, living as he does on the mountain tops seven months in the year and in complete isolation. With the big 'business house' of Government in Simla and the growing millions on the plains, there is a solid dead rock; and even the piercing cry of the feeble millions is broken into nothingness, as it heaves up to the mountain top from the plains."

¤　　¤　　¤

*In* The Oppression of the Poor *Andrews tells of a public meeting outdoors in a town in East Bengal where relief was gathered for the suffering people then still trapped in the camps of Chandpur. The story reads like a passage from one of the gospels; it could be called "the clothing of the five thousand." Andrews rejoices in this example of self-*

*giving and concern for others, yet in the midst of his account he confesses his dread of the return of violence.*

¤   ¤   ¤

On the first day of my arrival at Chittagong, a public meeting was held in the open air, in one of nature's amphitheaters. A high bank of grass in the background formed an excellent sitting place for thousands of people. The appeal was on behalf of the distressed and stranded labourers at Chandpur, and it was stated that they were in need of clothing. In a moment, the air was white with shawls and upper garments, which were thrown forward towards the platform. For a few seconds, as those on the grassy amphitheater stripped off their upper garments and threw them forward, the sight had almost the appearance of a fall of snow, so white it looked.

The sacrifice which was shown at that meeting had a powerful effect upon my own mind and I know that others felt it also. What everyone experienced was a sudden kindling of the heart, with joy to be present at such an auspicious moment. So intense was the psychological impression that those who had come, never intending to give, gave lavishly. They could not resist the wave of public feeling. The mass enthusiasm carried them beyond their conventional ideas.

That night, when I had retired to rest and was thinking it all over alone, I felt certain that I had been given a glimpse of insight into the hearts of the people of East Bengal who have lived (as their ancestors lived before them) in the presence of these great rivers and who have done their business, as the Psalmist says, "beside great waters." They have had to face dangers of storm and flood from childhood, and they have learnt to rely upon one another. I could feel their hearts beating warmly with love, and it touched me very deeply indeed. My own nature is impulsive, and I did not find it difficult to respond to their affection.

Yet, at the same time, a dread has not infrequently possessed me. In no part of India—not even in the Punjab, have I ever felt the danger of an actual outbreak of violence so near at hand as in East Bengal. Hitherto, this danger has been overcome even here. But violent speeches are being uttered, in spite of Mahatma Gandhi's warning. And so the question that I have been asking myself with great anxiety is, "Can the movement here be kept throughout free from violence of any kind?" Passionately I desire and pray that it may; but I cannot help asking the question anxiously.

¤  ¤  ¤

*The depth of Andrews' anxiety and concern would lead to his next public disagreement with Gandhi.*

# Chapter 6

## Violence or non-violence?

A ndrews' fears were increasingly realized as he saw a violent spirit entering the non-cooperation movement at the same time that the British were using increased force to quell popular uprisings. The poet Tagore's words expressed Andrews' own apprehension when he said of the popular excitement, "It shouts to me; it does not sing."

Gandhi was aware of the problem, but had to admit that even he was not "fully capable of controlling and disciplining the spirit of revolt," although he strenuously attempted to do so by exhortation and fasting. Yet Gandhi himself was employing a strategy that Andrews thought was dangerously blurring the line between violence and non-violence. His newest tactic was setting fire to great mounds of imported clothing.

In accordance with his swadeshi principle, Gandhi strongly believed that Indians should be producing and wearing only the homespun cloth called khaddar. By using his own spinning-wheel, he witnessed constantly to the importance *of promoting self-sufficiency in the villages. His followers, Andrews included, wore* khaddar *instead of British-made cloth. Now, by these bonfires of foreign cloth, he was bringing international as well as national attention to the issue of imports and the colonial dependency they created.*

*One can imagine the excitement when Gandhi kindled such bonfires on streets near the procession honoring the Prince of Wales during his visit to Bombay in November, 1921. As the flames leaped upwards so did the chants of "Mahatma Gandhi ki jai!" At the same time Congress had resolved to mark the Prince's visit with a national* hartal *and a boycott of ceremonies, but passions ran too high for an orderly protest. Street fighting broke out and many were killed in Bombay.*

*Just how deeply this development troubled Andrews may be seen in a public exchange of letters between himself and Gandhi in August and September of 1921. In his book* Mahatma Gandhi's Ideas, *Andrews introduces the letters with a strong statement of his own feelings.*

¤   ¤   ¤

A time came when I was drawn, much against my own will, into the controversy with regard to violent methods of action. For it seemed to me that Mahatma Gandhi was going much too far, and literally "playing with fire," when he himself took the lead in burning huge heaps of foreign clothes. Not only did it appear to me to carry with it a certain racial bitterness, which was foreign to his own pure nature, but also inevitably to lead on to further violence. Both in the public press and also by outward action, I felt bound to put forward my protest against this.

In answer to my own protest and to almost innumerable private letters, Mahatma Gandhi wrote the following article in *Young India*: "The reader will, I am sure, appreciate my sharing with him the following beautiful and pathetic letter from Mr. Andrews. He writes to me:

'I know that your burning of foreign cloth is with the idea of helping the poor, but I feel that you have gone wrong. There is a subtle appeal to racial feeling in that word "foreign" which day by day appears to need checking and not fomenting. The picture of your lighting that great pile, including delicate fabrics, shocked me intensely. We seem to be losing sight of the great outside world to which we belong and concentrating selfishly on India; and this must (I fear) lead back to the old, bad, selfish nationalism. If so, we get into the vicious circle from which Europe is trying so desperately to escape. But I cannot argue it out. I can only say again that it shocked me, and seemed to me a form of violence; and yet I know how violence is abhorrent to you. I do not at all like this question of foreign cloth being made into a religion.

I was supremely happy when you were dealing giant blows at the fundamental moral evils—drunkenness, drug-taking, untouchability, race arrogance, etc., and when you were, with such wonderful and beautiful tenderness, dealing with the hideous vice of prostitution. But lighting bonfires of foreign cloth and telling people that it is a religious sin to wear it; destroying in the fire that noble handiwork of one's own fellow men and women, of one's brothers and sisters abroad, saying it would be "defiling" to use it—I cannot tell you how different all this appears to me! Do you know I almost fear now to wear the *khaddar* that you have given me, lest I should appear to be judging other people, as a Pharisee would, saying, 'I am holier than thou!' I have never felt like this before.

You know how, when anything that you do hurts me, I must cry out to you, and this has hurt me.'

This is his letter.

It is so like him. Whenever he feels hurt over anything I have done—and this is by no means the first of such occasions—he deluges me with letters without waiting for an answer. For it is love speaking to love, not arguing. And so it has been over the burning of foreign clothes.

I remain just as convinced as ever of the necessity of burning. There is no emphasis, in the process, of race feeling. I would have done precisely the same thing in sacred and select family or friendly circles. In all I do or advise, the infallible test I apply is, whether the particular action will hold good in regard to the dearest and the nearest. The teaching of the faith I hold dear is unmistakable and unequivocal in the matter. I must be the same to friend and foe. And it is this conviction which makes me so sure of so many of my acts which often puzzle friends.

I remember having thrown into the sea a pair of beautiful field-glasses, because they were a constant bone of contention between a dear friend and myself. He felt the hesitation at first, but he saw the right of the destruction of a beautiful and costly thing, a present withal from a friend. Experience shows that the richest gifts must be destroyed without compensation and hesitation if they hinder one's moral progress. Will it not be held a sacred duty to consign to the flames most precious heirlooms, if they are plague-infected? I can remember having broken to bits, when a young man, the loved bangles of my own dear wife, because they were a matter of difference between us. And if I remember aright, they were a gift from her mother. I did it, not out of hate, but out of love—ignorant, I now see in my ripe age. The destruction helped us and brought us nearer.

If the emphasis were on all foreign things, it would be racial, parochial, and wicked. The emphasis is on all foreign cloth. The restriction makes all the difference in the world. I do not want to shut out English lever watches or the beautiful Japanese lacquer work. But I must destroy all the choicest wines of Europe, even though they might have been prepared and preserved with all the most exquisite care and attention.

Satan's snares are most subtly laid, and they are the most tempting, when the dividing line between right and wrong is so thin as to be imperceptible. But the line is there all the same, rigid and inflexible. Any crossing of it may mean certain death.

India is racial today. It is with the utmost effort that I find it possible to keep under check the evil passions of the people. The general body of the people are filled with ill will, because they are weak and hopelessly ignorant of the way to shed their weakness. I am transferring the ill will from men to things. Love of foreign cloth has brought foreign domination, pauperism, and what is worst, shame to many a home.

The reader may not know, that not long ago hundreds of "untouchable" weavers of Kathiawar, having found their calling gone, became sweepers for the Bombay municipality. And the life of these men has become so difficult that many lose their children and become physical and moral wrecks; some are helpless witnesses of the shame of their daughters and even their wives. The reader may not know that many women of this class in Gujarat, for want of domestic occupation having taken to work on public roads, under pressure of one sort or another, are obliged to sell their honour. The reader may not know that the proud weavers of the Punjab, for want of occupation, not many years ago, took to the sword, and were instrumental in killing the proud and innocent Arabs at the bidding of their officers, not for the sake of their country, but for the sake of their livelihood. It is difficult to make a successful appeal to those deluded hirelings and wean them from their murderous profession.

Is it any wonder if I consider it a sin to touch foreign cloth?

¤　　¤　　¤

*This was a very public disagreement. When he was invited by Gandhi to address a major gathering of the Indian National Congress in December, 1921, Andrews appeared*

*in a European suit in order to make his protest the more
visible.*

*Apart from the campaign to destroy foreign cloth,
Andrews had nothing but praise for Gandhi's efforts to keep
the movement non-violent. He wrote of the birth of a new
spirit in India, "infinitely beyond the servile spirit of the
past." One of the examples of this new spirit to which he
liked to point was something Andrews saw with his own
eyes in the Punjab in September, 1922. Sikhs demanding
the right to cut firewood in a garden near Amritsar controlled by religious officials adopted Gandhian tactics. They
went repeatedly to the gate of the garden and submitted
themselves to vicious beatings by the military police,
without offering a single blow in return.*

*Many of these men had fought in the war, but they were
now learning to fight a new kind of battle, which they called
"Mahatma Gandhi's battle." Andrews writes of visiting
them in the hospital on the day after their beatings were
inflicted, and how he saw a religious fervor in their faces as
they uttered Gandhi's name with great love. "When I asked
them whether they would be prepared to go through the
same suffering again, their faces lighted up with joy as they
answered "Yes."*

*Such was the potential of Gandhi's movement that even
Sikh warriors could learn non-violence. If we recall
Gandhi's argument with Andrews about military recruitment, we will remember Gandhi's claim that those trained
for war might make the best* satyagrahis! *All these things
seemed possible, yet late in 1921 it was the movement's
potential for violence that came to be realized more and
more. Here Andrews describes how even Gandhi's influence could no longer hold it to a peaceful course.*

¤   ¤   ¤

As the non-cooperation movement proceeded, the inherent defects in it became more pronounced. Its very popularity became its greatest hindrance. Mahatma Gandhi himself saw the dangers, and gave the warning again and again. But it was already too late. The excitement had gone too deep. The great masses of India had awakened to the sense of their own power without having received sufficient spiritual training to keep that power under control. There was nothing except his own personality, intense enough in its own inner quality, to retain a magnetic hold over the minds of the masses in their sudden awakening to their new acquisition of explosive freedom. He himself was able, for a time, amazingly to hold violence at bay. Along with his lieutenants he worked with superhuman energy in order to maintain control. But the excitement of the times, and the excessive strain caused by daily overwork, made the leaders themselves unaware of the pace at which the current was driving the frail boat of their national endeavour towards the rapids. There were two or three premonitory warnings, and then the crash came at Bombay [during the Prince of Wales' visit in November 1921], when violence raged day after day in the city almost unchecked, in spite of heroic efforts to prevent it.

During all these last tumultuous days I had been called away from India to Kenya and South Africa, and had come back into the midst of the confusion at the end of the Bombay Riots. Mahatma Gandhi had gone through his act of penance and self-purification. His high courage had not left him, but he looked haggard and emaciated, as one who had just passed through the valley of the shadow of death. Indeed, to die would have been to him, at such a time as this, an infinite release. But it was not to happen.

During the months that followed, his efforts toward creating non-violence in the atmosphere of non-cooperation were ever more incessant. He wore himself out with tireless activity by day and with sleepless watch and prayer by night. Only a spirit like the finest tempered steel could have stood such a test of endurance. Then the second outbreak of violence came at Chauri Chaura.

¤   ¤   ¤

*On February 5, 1922, at Chauri Chaura in the United Provinces, mob violence resulted in the brutal murders of twenty-one policemen. They were hacked to death and their remains thrown into a blazing fire.*

*When he heard of it Gandhi immediately gave orders to call off the entire campaign. "If we are not to evolve violence out of non-violence, it is quite clear that we must hastily retrace our steps and re-establish an atmosphere of peace, rearrange our programme and not think of starting mass civil disobedience until we are sure of peace being retained."*

*Once again, as with Amritsar, Gandhi had initiated a mass protest only to call it off abruptly. A successful campaign of* satyagraha *demanded the utmost in personal discipline and self-control; without it, the campaign disintegrated into mob violence. Even though the Viceroy seemed ready to negotiate with Gandhi as a result of a successful tax strike then gathering momentum throughout the Gujarat, Gandhi insisted on abandoning a campaign which was to him a moral failure. He was bitterly attacked by many of his coworkers for this decision, but praised by Andrews, who called this outward defeat Gandhi's greatest moral triumph.*

*What a triumph it was would be revealed in the course of Gandhi's trial in March of 1922. Arrested at his ashram for his leadership of the non-cooperation campaign, Gandhi appeared before the magistrate in Ahmedabad eight days later. Unfortunately, Andrews could not be with him; living with striking railway workers in Tundla, he was hard at work attempting to bring their strike against the East India Railway to a peaceful end. Gandhi insisted that Andrews not abandon that important work to come to be with him.*

*In what has been called one of the great trials in history, Gandhi was charged with "exciting disaffection towards His Majesty's Government." He entered a plea of guilty, for he regarded such disaffection to be a virtue, yet he spoke in open court with complete frankness about the violence which he had not been able to control and asked for the full penalty of the law.*

¤   ¤   ¤

I wish to endorse all the blame that the learned Advocate-General has thrown on my shoulders in connection with the Bombay occurrences, Madras occurrences, and the Chauri Chaura occurrences. Thinking over these deeply and sleeping over them night after night, it is impossible for me to dissociate myself from the diabolical crimes of Chauri Chaura or the mad outrages of Bombay. He is quite right when he says that as a man of responsibility, a man having received a fair share of education, having had a fair share of experience of this world, I should have known the consequences of every one of my acts. I knew that I was playing with fire. I ran the risk, and if I was set free, I would still do the same. I have felt it this morning that I would have failed in my duty if I did not say what I said here just now.

I wanted to avoid violence. non-violence is the first article of my faith. It is also the last article of my creed. But I had to make my choice. I had either to submit to a system which I considered had done an irreparable harm to my country, or incur the risk of the mad fury of my people bursting forth, when they understood the truth from my lips. I know that my people have sometimes gone mad. I am deeply sorry for it and I am therefore here to submit not to a light penalty but to the highest penalty. I do not ask for mercy. I do not plead any extenuating act. I am here, therefore, to invite and cheerfully submit to the highest penalty that can be inflicted upon me for what in law is a deliberate crime and what appears to me to be the highest duty of a citizen.

¤    ¤    ¤

*He was sentenced by the judge, who could not help but greatly admire him, to serve six years in prison. Even in confinement, Gandhi refused to ask for any special treatment. One consequence, writes a biographer, was that "even C. F. Andrews was unable to come to see him." So that his friend would not worry, however, Gandhi wrote him to say, "I am as happy as a bird."*

*He found a Chinese Christian friend in Yeravda Prison with whom he could study the Bible in the evenings; during the day Gandhi read the* Gita, *on which he wrote a commentary. He also wrote an account of the* satyagraha *movement, began his autobiography, spun hundreds of yards of cloth, read British authors such as Kipling, Jules Verne, and Gibbon!*

*Still his health deteriorated, and Gandhi's prison term came to an end after less than two years. Following an emergency operation for a suppurating appendix that nearly caused his death, he was unconditionally released in January, 1924, and sent to recuperate at a hospital in Poona. Andrews, who had been in England for medical treatment himself, came quickly to his friend's side when he heard of his illness. There began then the closest and most intimate period of their friendship, a period of calm and relative tranquillity for Gandhi that was to continue for four more years.*

# Chapter 7

## The Gift of Peace

For two months Andrews lived with Gandhi in Juhu, on the seacoast not far from Bombay, during his convalescence in 1924. Since for Gandhi this was a time of recuperation, with at least a relative release from work, what Andrews writes about this period gives us our best picture of the discipline of prayer and meditation which undergirded all that Gandhi did. We also learn from these writings of Andrews' own search for peace and balance in his sometimes driven life.

The scene at Juhu had its comic side, as was usually the case wherever Gandhi resided. He was in the habit of inviting ailing friends to visit him and then subjecting them to mud packs, water baths, food fads, and massages to restore them to health. But it was the health of the independence movement that most needed his attention at this time, for during his twenty-two months in prison the movement had foundered in a number of important ways.

*The boycott of the legislative councils had had unfortunate results, for those still remaining on the councils were not supporters of the independence movement and the laws they passed might harm the cause. Congress had split on this question, with the Swaraj Party urging that Congress members be elected to the councils to be in closer touch with the people and able to resist the British from within. This view prevailed, although Gandhi opposed it at first, and Andrews complained of "wrecking tactics" by some of the Swaraj leaders.*

*Larger problems emerged: religious intolerance in the Punjab, terrorist activities in Bengal, and a general loss of discipline within the independence movement. Gandhi's prescription was a renewed commitment to* khaddar *and to unity work. He appealed to all to rally around the flag, which bore the colors of communal unity, and the* charkha, *or spinning wheel.*

*Many came to consult with Gandhi about tactics and alliances; Andrews took part in all of these consultations and edited* Young India *for him as well. But in the following article, written for the* Atlantic Monthly *and entitled "A Day with Mahatma Gandhi," it is the centrality of prayer and meditation in the austere and simple life at Juhu that he emphasizes. Here Andrews presents Gandhi as the one who can bring healing to the movement because he is in touch with the source of healing within.*

¤   ¤   ¤

Perhaps the simple detailed account of a single day with Mahatma Gandhi during his convalescence will, more than anything else, bring the Western reader much nearer to the heart of things in India. It may possibly, at the same time, leave him somewhat bewildered at the subtle differences of mental temperament which are so fascinating, and yet so baffling to trace down to their ultimate source. Without any question, in the East the power of religion over life has marvelously persisted. The "Ages of Faith" are still being lived; and India is, above all others, the country where spirit rules over matter in the modern world. This is the deepest difference of all between East and West, and it is seen in Mahatma Gandhi most distinctly.

The day begins very early. At 4 a.m. the household assembles. We remain seated on mats upon the floor of the verandah in perfect silence. Sometimes the moon is shining through the waving palm trees outside. On other mornings all is dark. After the silence there follow Sanskrit verses, chanted in a monotone, and a hymn from some mediaeval saint. Then silence once more for a short time while we remain seated and after each retires. Our united worship is now over. Each one goes apart and strict silence will be observed until the sun rises in the east.

I would mention, in a parenthesis, that prolonged early morning meditation is no unusual habit in India. With the poet, Rabindranath Tagore, it has become a natural custom to begin the day with this inner silence a very long time before the dawn. Often he thus enters upon the day soon after two o'clock in the morning and sits in silence till seven. It is the only way, he has told me, that the spirit can be controlled in all its moods and be made ready for the trials of the day. Others, whom I know well, have given me similar accounts of the process of their daily lives, by which the mastery of the soul is reached in the early dawn through meditation and silence.

Among the Sanskit verses, recited in our household prayers with Mahatma Gandhi, are the following from the *Bhagavad Gita*:

That man alone is wise,

Who keeps the mastery of himself! If one

Ponders on objects of the sense, there springs
Attraction; from attraction grows desire.
Desire flames to fierce passion . . .
But if one deals with objects of the sense,
Not loving and not hating, making them
Serve his free soul, which rests serenely, lord,
Lo! such a man comes to tranquillity.

And like the ocean, day by day receiving
Floods from all lands, which never overflows:
Its boundary-line not leaping, and not leaving,
Fed by the rivers, but unswelled by those,

So is the perfect one! To his soul's ocean,
The world of sense pours streams of witchery;
They leave him as they find, without commotion,
Taking their tribute, but remaining sea.

As I have read that passage over and over again, it has given me an insight into the true mind and character of the East. Mahatma Gandhi carries out its precepts to the fullest extent. It remains ever the highest ideal to be reached; the pearl of great price, for which a man will sell all that he has, if only he may obtain it.

About seven o'clock in the morning Mahatma Gandhi has some milk and fruit. This is his staple food throughout the day even when he is well. Very soon after this, Pandit Radhakanta Malaviya arrives with his two little children carrying some white blossoms. The blossoms are laid at the Mahatma's feet, and then the little ones run into his arms. They are not in the least afraid of the Hindu saint, who is very human where children are concerned. A portion of the Ramayana is read and studied on the roof. The sea murmurs on the beach and the palm trees wave their leaves backward and forward gently in the morning breeze. At eight o'clock this quiet time is broken. An endless tide of visitors begins to flow toward him. Each comes for advice; and it is strange to note how the political issues always take a philosophical turn before many minutes are over. This does not mean that the solution offered is any the less practical; but while the English mind quite naturally and instinctively looks to the immediate effect in politics, the Indian mind with equal naturalness of instinct looks to the remoter springs of action.

On two days in the week Mahatma Gandhi maintains complete silence. For he is the editor of two weekly papers, and he writes his editorials on these silent days. One of these papers is called *Young India*, and it is probably the most remarkable weekly newspaper in the world today. It contains no advertisements, but only page after page from the editor's exhaustless spring of new ideas written in compact English sentences with not a superfluous word. The other paper, called the *Nava Jivan* (New Life), printed in Gujarati and Hindi, has by far the largest circulation. It is his pet child and he lavishes his best energies upom it. Even without advertisements its net profits had come to fifty thousand rupees a short time ago, all of which were handed over to the National Congress.

At noon he usually takes a very short rest for half an hour, but this is often made impossible by visitors. A full hour is given afterward by him to his son in teaching him Gujarati literature. Then he sits down to the spinning. For to him the economic salvation of his country through the spinning wheel has become more than a mere doctrine. This ideal of his, that India should thus win her salvation, is a pure and passionate faith wherewith his very life has become enriched and enlarged. He inspires with his own enthusiasm anyone who comes within the orbit of his attraction. In spite of the fact that the doctor had forbidden spinning so soon after his serious illness, he found that he could not keep away from it any longer; and even though it may tire him physically it is certainly a great relief to the mental strain of the day.

That strain becomes the hardest to bear in the evening. For the crowd will insist on gathering in large numbers, and among them are always the poorest of the poor. For those poor people his sympathies are ever ready to be given to the fullest limit of his endurance. But when the time of sunset comes, sheer physical weariness at last makes even his indomitable spirit yield before its urgent demand for rest. A short walk, very slowly, along the beach at sunset, the evening prayers, and again the silence of meditation—these bring the long day to a close. He sleeps well and thus recuperates his strength.

Since this was written, Mahatma Gandhi, all too soon, has left his home of convalescence by the seaside and has returned to his own ashram, or religious retreat, at Sabarmati, where his work is far more strenous. From that place he is now directing the whole Indian movement along the pathway of nonviolence.

¤　　¤　　¤

*Andrews' gift of religious insight lay in his ability to see in other religious traditions what was of greatest importance in his own. In this description of the day with Gandhi we can see how Gandhi becomes for Andrews a reflection of Christ—the Christ of the gospels who took the little children in his arms. The crowds press in on Gandhi and he withdraws from time to time to renew his strength, much as Jesus did. Gandhi's teachings, too, would strike familiar chords for Andrews from the gospels and epistles.*

*Consider this passage from Gandhi's commentary on the* Bhagavad Gita *concerning true devotion, recalling that*

*Andrews had borrowed a phrase from the gospels to call this ideal of Hinduism "the pearl of great price."*

¤    ¤    ¤

He is the devotee who is jealous of none, who is a fount of mercy, who is without egotism, who is selfless, who treats alike cold and heat, happiness and misery, who is ever forgiving, who is always contented, whose resolutions are firm, who has dedicated mind and soul to God, who causes no dread, who is not afraid of others, who is free from exultation, sorrow and fear, who is pure, who is versed in action and yet remains unaffected by it, who renounces all fruit, good or bad, who treats friend and foe alike, who is untouched by respect or disrespect, who is not puffed up by praise, who does not go under when people speak ill of him, who loves silence and solitude, who has a disciplined reason. Such devotion is inconsistent with the existence at the same time of strong attachments.

We thus see that to be a real devotee is to realize oneself. Self-realization is not something apart. One rupee can purchase for us poison or nectar, but knowledge or devotion cannot buy us either salvation or bondage. These are not media of exchange. They are themselves the things we want. In other words, if the means and the end are not identical, they are almost so. The extreme of means is salvation. Salvation of the Gita is perfect peace.

¤    ¤    ¤

*Andrews wrote another description of a time of prayer with Gandhi, this time at Gandhi's own Sabarmati ashram. In this account he makes a connection between prayer and the service of the poor, since God's presence is revealed in each activity. Here is another instance of Andrews' ability to recognize in Hinduism a truth he had first discovered in the teachings of Christ, who identified himself with the poor when he said: "Inasmuch as ye did it unto one of the least of these, ye did it unto me."*

*Andrews had learned from Gandhi a similar story in the Hindu scriptures, where God also is worshiped in the form of a poverty-stricken man. In that story the Divine Being appears in the guise of a poor man begging for food and is recognized by a devout person, who sees through the outward form to the God hidden within.*

*In this time of prayer Andrews describes at Sabarmati, the identity of God with the poor is focused by means of a poem by his other great friend and teacher, Rabindranath Tagore.*

¤   ¤   ¤

Even to this day I can remember the evening, at the sunset hour of prayer, when we were seated at our devotions on the bank of the Sabarmati River at Mahatma Gandhi's ashram, and he asked me to read some poem from Tagore. It was the poem quoted here that I read, and it seemed to me that in the company of Mahatma Gandhi and his chosen band of followers the presence of God was almost visibly near at hand in the cool of the day there in that Ashram where the poor were so loved and revered.

Long years afterwards I heard Mahatma Gandhi in a deeply moving way refer to that evening worship and that reading from Rabindranath Tagore, and I realized that he had felt, as I had on that occasion, the mysterious presence of the Eternal.

Here is Thy footstool and there rest Thy feet where live the poorest and lowliest and the lost.

When I try to bow to Thee, my obeisance cannot reach down to the depth where Thy feet rest among the poorest and lowliest and lost.

Pride can never approach to where Thou walkest in the clothes of the humble among the poorest and lowliest and lost.

My heart can never find its way to where Thou keepest company with the companionless among the poorest, the lowliest, and the lost.

¤   ¤   ¤

*Andrews received the gift of peace in India, where he had numerous teachers in the art of prayer and contemplation. Three who were most important to him were Gandhi, the poet Tagore and Susil Rudra, his colleague at St. Stephen's College in Delhi. What he learned from them in India Andrews would share later with many in the West, especial ly in the 1930s, when he traveled widely lecturing and writing about the spiritual life.*

*In a book from that period entitled* The Inner Life, *he describes his pilgrimage, contrasting the pace of his former life in London, where he worked tirelessly, at times franti- cally, for the poor, with his new life in India.*

¤   ¤   ¤

When I first came to India, one of the welcome and wholesome changes in my life was the relief from strain because the pace of daily life was slower. In England, I had begun to grudge every moment of the day that was not spent on active service among the poor; each day became crowded with engagements, but my own prayer life suffered grievous harm. It required a time of quiet in the East before I could realize how unbalanced my life had become. Susil Kumar Rudra had learnt how to retire within himself. No one could be with him for long without feeling the atmosphere of peace which encompassed his life. He would smile at my over-eager- ness to "get things done," and warn me that in the East impatience was an evil and not a virtue.

113

During the college vacation each year we used to go together into the heart of the Himalayas. These periods of rest in the mountains made clear to me that the inner life, with its profound humility, has the first place; if these qualities are absent, outward activities are of no account. As we came near Narkanda on our journey into the hills, the distant mountains would come suddenly into view. At sunset, the whole horizon was flushed with gold; the scene was like a city in the sky, with walls and gates and towers, like the "Heavenly City" in the Book of Revelation, where the writer says, describing his "dream":

I, John, saw the Holy City, New Jerusalem,

Coming down from God out of heaven,

Prepared as a bride adorned for her husband.

In the sunset were all the jewelled colours mentioned in the Book of Revelation. The billowy mists appeared like "a great multitude of the heavenly host." God, the great Artificer, seemed to be painting anew with his many colours the mountains and the clouds, which every moment seemed to change their forms and shapes in the changing light.

When I went to live with the poet Rabindranath Tagore at Santiniketan in the depth of the country in Bengal, life became still more restful for me. Much of the quiet at Santiniketan was learnt during silent walks alone over the open country, which stretched far and wide on almost every side. When Susil was with me, he would share these walks, and his good counsel was ever ready to help me in difficult situations. We would also sit together for long hours in the cool of the evening after the sun had gone down, while the stars came out one by one. Nowhere in the whole world is night more beautiful than in India, where for more than half the year the sky is almost cloudless, and the moon and the stars are visible in all their glory.

Mahatma Gandhi helped me to overcome my restlessness by encouraging me to retire early in the evening, in order to get up before sunrise each morning. Both in Santiniketan and South Africa, the habit of rising before dawn for quiet and prayer became more and more normal with me, and this brought strength and healing with it, even when the hardest problems had to be faced throughout the day. This morning quiet has become a necessary part of my daily life and has often saved me from disaster.

This gift of peace remained with me on long sea journeys which I had to undertake. There is a quiet on board ship when the open sky with its myriad stars overhead and the still ocean below seems to be the symbol of two immensities between which the spirit of man is poised both in space and time. The monotonous lap of the waves against the side of the ship seems only to add to the stillness. Thus, little by little, instead of the old strained feeling, a new restfulness came flowing in.

When I came back to the West after living so many years in the East what struck me most of all was the pace at which human life had been "speeded up." There is, among the young, a peculiar pleasure in this enhanced speed. Fine courage and daring faith seem to wrapped up with it, and these always appeal to the temperament of youth. Yet there was also much feverish anxiety and strain. When *What I Owe To Christ* was published, letters began to come asking for help. "Teach us," they said, "how to pray." I knew that this personal experience of mine in the East had been a talent given me by God which was intended to be used. If I had remained in England my inner life would have had none of these great fresh draughts of peace which were so lavishly bestowed on me in the East.

The great need of the human spirit, whether it be in America or Australia, is for the recovery of that simplicity, which is one of the foundations of true childlike faith. Like the man in the

Gospel story, who "had great possessions" which he was not willing to surrender, so, today, the modern world has its own "great possessions" of a strangely new character, which it will not yield up for Christ's sake. It must have its cinema, its radio, its motor, and its aeroplane. It must also have its money to purchase comfort and to keep up its "high" standard of living. But when these so entirely absorb the attention that there is no place left for prayer and very little consideration for the poor, then there must be something terribly wrong with the life of the soul. The great renunciation will not be made; for these inventions have then become a part of life itself, as one of its driving forces. These new worldly riches and comforts, of whatever kind they are, keep the heart of man fixed upon the surface of things, the externals of life, so that he becomes dependent on them, while that which is spiritual withers away for lack of use.

I was able to give some of these thoughts at first hand, because my life had been spent in the East and I had learnt from it. When I spoke about these things, there was a wholehearted and immediate response, combined with a sincere humility, which touched me very deeply indeed.

¤　　¤　　¤

*There were many who testified to the inner peace which they sensed in Andrews' life, even in the midst of strenuous activities. Gandhi wrote to a mutual friend: "Like his economy, Andrews' purdah [seclusion] is a fraud! He pretends that he needs quiet for his writing, and then sits down to write in the midst of bustle and produces quiet from within."*

*Yet Gandhi also knew how anxious Charlie could still become. Peace and a sense of God's presence was by no means a constant possession for him. "I have no continuous, untroubled faith," he wrote. "'A little while and ye shall see me, and again a little while and ye shall not see me' is very real to me."*

Andrews quite freely confesses his bouts of anxiety in The Inner Life. *Characteristically, these bouts of worry were not for himself and his own difficulties.*

¤ ¤ ¤

I have had for a long time a constant nervous anxiety about other people—especially those who are near to me—which makes it difficult for me entirely to leave them in God's own loving keeping as I ought to do. Instead of this, I often become so nervous about them that the anxiety seems for a time to get the better of me and to fill my mind with useless alarms and fears. As long as it lasts, the strain on the nerves becomes acute; and the inner peace, that is so ample at other times, is then lost for the time being. When I wrote about this, as a weakness which I would never wish to hide, I stated that it was possible to look back and say with thankfulness that it had been partly overcome. That was nearly six years ago; yet even now the complete victory has not been given to me, and I have once more to acknowledge this partial inward defeat. But I should be a poor Christian, if I yielded on that account to despair, or gave up the struggle.

{} {} {}

*Of course Andrews often worried about Gandhi over the years, in all of his trials and tribulations. Gandhi's response to Andrews' fears was to try to minister to his friend's anxiety with humor. One letter begins: "My dear Charlie, No letter from you means no anxiety complex." And in one of those brief but revealing cables they sent to each other, we read: All Well. Anxiety Complex Not Allowed. Love. Mohan.*

*Later in the year 1924, after his stay with Gandhi at Juhu, Andrews traveled to Malaya and Burma, where he was investigating the conditions of Indian labor. When he submitted his impressions of Burma for publication in Young India, Gandhi chided him, as only he could, for working too hard and disrupting that very balance between work and prayer Andrews praised so highly.*

¤    ¤    ¤

25 August 1924

Dear Charlie,

I have read your article on Burma. The thing is shocking. You have seen too much to enable you to analyze properly and trace causes. Moreover, you have not had enough time to study each problem. Will you not rest and be thankful for a while? Work is prayer but it can also be madness . . . I am printing it nevertheless because it comes from the utmost purity of your heart.

With love deeper than even you can fathom,<br>
Yours,<br>
Mohan

# Chapter 8

## The Great Fast

The summer of 1924 was a time of great communal strife. Tensions between Hindus and Muslims had been building since a Muslim uprising in 1924 in Malabar, when thousands of Hindus were massacred or forced to convert to Islam. In the large cities, competition for jobs increased. Muslims found themselves at a disadvantage, since Hindus and Christians had better educational opportunities and inside connections that led to advancement. Religious differences were exacerbated, too, particularly as Hindus took offence at the Muslim slaughter of cattle. Gandhi pointed out that this was unfair; the British had done the same for many years without creating such resentment, and riots in the name of the sacred cow were for him "an insane waste of effort." But the voice of sanity could not be heard. There were almost daily reports of violent confrontations, especially in the north of India.

Predictably, the response of government authorities to the turmoil was extremely aggressive. This increase in turmoil was easily interpreted by the British as sufficient justification in itself for both their presence and their repressive acts.

Gandhi was deeply troubled and shamed by this open violation of the unity he had hoped to instill in the Indian people. He appealed to both sides to end the violence, and although his appeals had some effect, he finally determined to undertake a major fast for the sake of the unity of his people and his movement.

It would be a fast of twenty-one days. Having recently recovered from a serious illness, underweight—he would weigh only eighty-eight pounds by the end of the fast—and fifty-six years old, it was clear that Gandhi might not survive it. The prospective fast was, then, a sacrificial act; his hope was that it might establish a spiritual bond between himself and the perpetrators of violence that could cause a change of heart. But it was also an act of self-purification for the sins that he had unwittingly committed, for the violence that had followed upon his experiments in non-cooperation. "It is both a penance and a prayer," Gandhi said.

The prayer was for unity, without which, he believed, India could never achieve her independence. The effect of the fast was electric, felt across the length and breadth of the land. It became known as "the Great Fast." It was a dramatic political act, and at the same time a profoundly spiritual one. Andrews would meditate long on its spiritual meaning, coming to see in Gandhi a reflection of the Christ who bears the sins of his people in his own body.

Gandhi wrote to Andrews from Delhi on September 17, 1924, to announce his intention to fast.

¤   ¤   ¤

My dearest Charlie,

Don't you fret over my decision. It has been taken after deep prayer and clearest possible indication. This fast of twenty-one days is the least I can do. Oh, the agony of it all! Every day has been a day of torture. But I shall soon be at peace. I was longing to see my duty clearly. The light has come like a flash. Can a man do more than give his life?

With dearest love,

Yours,

Mohan

¤ ¤ ¤

*Andrews went to Delhi immediately in order to be at Gandhi's side, to edit his paper, and to shield him from the press of visitors during the fast. He was uniquely fitted to be Gandhi's doorkeeper at such a time because, as he told a friend, people would obey his directions, knowing that he took on this responsibility "out of pure love."*

*Andrews' presence in Delhi also enabled him to participate in the "Unity Conference" that took place at the time of the fast. Four hundred religious figures from every religion and every province of India took part in this public attempt to heal India's divisions.*

*Here, in Gandhi's own words, we learn why he fasted, and how he understood his act as a penance for his own sins and those of the Hindu and Muslim rioters.*

¤ ¤ ¤

Have I erred, have I been impatient, have I compromised with evil? I may have done all these things or none of them. All I know is what I see before me. If real non-violence and truth had been practiced by the people who are now fighting, the gory duelling that is now going on would have been impossible. My responsibility is clearly somewhere.

I was violently shaken by the riots at Amethi, Sambhar, and Gulbarga. I had read the reports about Amethi and Sambar prepared by Hindu and Muslim friends. I had learnt the joint findings of Hindu and Muslim friends who went to Gulbarga. I was writhing in deep pain, and yet I had no remedy. The news of Kohat set the smouldering mass aflame. Something had got to be done. I passed two nights in restlessness and pain. On Wednesday I knew the remedy—I must do penance. In the ashram at the time of morning prayer we ask Shiva, God of Mercy, to forgive our sins knowingly or unknowingly committed. My penance is the prayer of a bleeding heart for forgiveness for sins unwittingly committed.

It is a warning to the Hindus and Muslims who have professed to love me. If they have loved me truly, and if I have been deserving of their love, they will do penance with me for the grave sin of denying God in their hearts. To revile one another's religion, to make reckless statements, to utter untruth, to break the heads of innocent men, to desecrate temples or mosques, is a denial of God. The world is watching—some with glee and some with sorrow—the dog-fight that is proceeding in our midst. We have listened to Satan. Religion— call it by what name you like—is made of sterner stuff. The penance of Hindus and Muslims is not fasting, but retracing their steps. It is true penance for a Muslim to harbour no ill for his Hindu brother, and an equally true penance for a Hindu to harbour none for his Muslim brother.

I ask of no Hindu or Muslim to surrender an iota of his religious principle. Only let him be sure that it is religion. But I do ask of every Hindu and Muslim not to fight for an earthly gain. I should be deeply hurt if my fast made either community surrender on a matter of principle. My fast is a matter between God and myself.

¤   ¤   ¤

*In a newspaper editorial which was widely read at the
time, Andrews gave a dramatic account of the fast. He
begins by setting the scene in Delhi against a backdrop of
Indian history. He points to two landmarks in the city. The
first recalls a fabled time of peace and religious tolerance
there during the reign of King Asoka (274-237 B.C.E.).
Asoka was a Buddhist convert who practiced* ahimsa *and
renounced armed conquest. Andrews contrasts this long-
gone era with the more recent history of Delhi. A memorial
to the Mutiny of 1857 brings memories of the bloody siege
and subsequent massacre in the city during the revolt of the
Bengal native army against the British.*

¤   ¤   ¤

At the foot of the ridge at Delhi, on the farther side away
from the city, is a house called Dil-khush, or Heart's Joy, where
Mahatma Gandhi had been keeping his fast. Above the house
stands out the historic ridge itself with its crumbling ruins telling
of many battles in days gone by. A "Mutiny Memorial" stands
at its highest point.

From the terrace on the upper story of Dil-khush there can
be seen ruined buttresses and walls, and not far away from
them Asoka's Pillar points its finger to the sky. In the darkness
of the night these landmarks stand out in the starlight and
against the moon. Between the ridge and the house below,
where Mahatma Gandhi lies in silence day by day, suffering
and exhausted, lines of motor-cars in the Delhi season block
the road each afternoon, while the golfers play their rounds of
golf.

Mahatma Gandhi had called me to the terrace one afternoon. Some musicians had come, and he wished me to hear
the music. It was one of his worst days; his weakness was

extreme. A boy was singing softly at the far end of the terrace. As I passed in order to sit down and listen to the music, I could not but take note how drawn the face of the sufferer was with pain. The sight renewed my anxiety, and at first I hardly listened to the music. The sun was setting in the west, and shafts of light were pouring from it, piercing the open glades where the golfers were busily playing their rounds of golf. The rocks and ruins on the hilltop were flushed with crimson and gold.

At last the beauty of the sky arrested me and soothed my inner fears; and then, as I looked towards the ridge, there appeared to come before my imagination the whole story of the past. That pillar, with its edict of toleration and non-violence, brought to my mind the Buddhist Age and the saintly King Asoka. The people of the land in those days were kindly and tolerant towards man and beast. It was an age of peace.

But those fortress ruins with the Mutiny Memorial told me of another chapter in human history, filled with bloodshed and bitter strife. On that evening the sun was setting peacefully in the west; but all through the previous night the ridge had been lashed by rain and tempest, and the winds had fiercely raged. The thunder had rolled along its sides and echoed in its rocks and hollows, and the jagged lightning had played against its summit. Even so, in Indian history the calm beauty of those peaceful days of King Asoka had been followed by the storm-swept days of war. Last of all, in the Mutiny the ridge had been stained with human blood and scarred by shot and shell.

Below the summit of the ridge, in the open spaces where the modern golf links had been made, I watched the golfers come and go. The clubs were swung and the balls were hit; muscular men and women marched forward, while little boys carried their golf clubs behind. Physical activity was there in every limb—physical and temporal power.

Instinctively my gaze turned back to the frail, wasted, tortured spirit on the terrace by my side, bearing the sins and sorrows of his people. With a rush of emotion there came to memory the passage from the Book of Lamentations—"Is it nothing to you, all ye that pass by? Behold and see, if there is any sorrow like unto my sorrow." And in that hour of vision I knew more deeply, in my own personal life, the meaning of the cross.

¤   ¤   ¤

*In commenting on these words of Andrews, the missionary writer E. Stanley Jones remarks that Gandhi's act was viewed similarly by Hindus. Setting Gandhi's act of sacrifice in its fullest Christian context, a leader of the national movement said to Jones, "I never understood what you missionaries were talking about until I saw the meaning of the cross in Gandhi."*

*For the last day of the fast Gandhi had devised an interfaith liturgy in order to bring his action to its proper conclusion. Andrews was called upon to witness to the power of the cross of Christ, and he did so by singing for Gandhi his favorite Christian hymn.*

¤   ¤   ¤

In the evening of the day before the fast was broken, Mahatma Gandhi was wonderfully bright and cheerful. Many of his most intimate friends came to see him as he lay upon his bed on the open roof of the house, which was flooded by the moonlight. It was only four days before the full moon.

The time came for evening prayers. As usual he called everyone who was in the house, including the Congress volunteers in attendance, to join him in the evening worship. The passage from the *Bhagavad Gita*, which is recited every night at Sabarmati Ashram, was said in unison. It tells about the complete conquest of the soul over the body's senses and appetites. At its close it speaks of the blessed peace in the heart of the one who conquers. As I looked at that bright face before me I could well understand the meaning of the words that were being recited.

After the Gita one of Kabir's hymns was sung by Balkrishna. Later on the same evening I asked for a translation, and I was told that Kabir in his hymn sings as a penitent to God, calling himself the chief of sinners. In God alone is his refuge. From experience I had learnt that hymns in this mood gave him most pleasure of all during his penance and fast. A very wonderful exposition of the Katha Upanishad followed by Vinoba, then a long silence. The friends parted one by one and he was left alone.

Before four o'clock in the morning of the next day we were called for the morning prayers. There was no moon and it was very dark. A chill breeze was blowing from the east. The morning star was shining in a clear open sky above the ridge. The phantom shapes of trees that rustled in the wind could be seen from the open room where we were all seated. He was wrapped warm in a dark shawl, and I asked him whether he had slept well. He replied, "Yes, very well indeed!" It was a happiness to notice at once that his voice was stronger than the morning before, instead of weaker. It would be difficult to describe the emotion of that silence which followed on this last day of the long fast, as we sat there waiting for all the household to assemble. We were all remembering that the final day had come. All the windows of the room where he was resting were open, and I sat gazing now at the figure reclining darkly upon the bed and now out at the stars.

The hymn that was sung at this special morning worship was one that was a great favourite with Mahatmaji. It is in Gujarati. What it says is this: "The way to God is only meant for heroes: it is not meant for cowards. There must be self-abandonment to the full. Only those who are ready to give up all for His sake can attain. As the diver dives down into the sea for pearls, even so heroic souls dive deep in their search for God."

After the prayers the early morning hours passed very quietly indeed; but before eight o'clock a very large number of visitors had begun to arrive. Some went away again after being allowed to see him; others stayed on, waiting till the fast was broken. At about 10 a.m. he called for me and said: "Can you remember the words of my favourite Christian hymn?"

I said: "Yes, shall I sing it to you now?"

"Not now," he answered, "but I have in my mind that when I break my fast we might have a little ceremony, expressing religious unity. I should like the Imam Sahib to recite the opening verses of the Quran. Then I would like you to sing the Christian hymn; you know the one I mean. It begins,

When I survey the wondrous cross

On which the Prince of Glory died—

and it ends,

Love so amazing, so divine,

Demands my soul, my life, my all.

And then, last of all, I should like Vinoba to recite from the Upanishads, and Balkrishna to sing the Vaishnava hymn describing the true Vaishnava."

When I had gone downstairs I told Krishnadas about the arrangements. He was very ill that day and I knew that it would give him great happiness to be able to keep the ceremony in spirit with us, though he could not be there in body before noon. All the leaders and friends had assembled. The ladies also were present who had loved to do him service. As the time drew near I went upstairs again, and he asked me to see to it personally that every one should be allowed to be present, including the servants of the house. Before this, quite early in the day, I had brought up the sweeper to see him, who had been serving us very faithfully, and he had spoken to him some very kindly words and had given him a smile of gratitude for the services he had rendered.

Now, at last, the midday hour had come and the fast was to be broken. The doctors were called first by themselves, and he gave them the most touching words of thanks for all their love and devotion to him. Hakim Ajmal Khan was called, who had also cheered and helped him through his fast as a doctor and friend. Maulana Mahomed Ali, his most tender and loving host, followed, and without any further order all went quietly into his room and greeted him with affection and sat down. The ladies who were present sat near the bedside. Swami Shraddhananda sat at the foot of the bed with his eyes closed in prayer.

The Imam Sahib, who had been one of his closest companions in South Africa and at Sabarmati Ashram, recited the wonderful Arabic opening words of the Quran, chanting its majestic language, which tells of God the Compassionate and Merciful, the Creator and Sustainer of the universe and the Helper of mankind. It ends with the prayer for His help to be guided in the path of righteousness and not in the way of sinners. After this, as had been arranged, the Christian hymn was sung. I quote the last two verses:

See from His head, His hands, His feet
Sorrow and love flow mingling down;
Did e'er such love and sorrow meet
Or thorns compose so rich a crown?
Were the whole realm of Nature mine
That were an offering far too small;
Love so amazing, so divine,
Demands my soul, my life, my all.

Then followed some very beautiful passages from the Upanishads, which were recited by Vinoba. Three of the slokas may be translated thus:—

> Those alone can realize the Divine Light within who have purified themselves through the constant practice of truth, self-discipline, meditation, and continence.
>
> By ceaseless pursuit of truth the Rishis of old attained their goal, even the supreme Truth.
>
> Let not my words belie my thoughts, nor my thoughts belie my words. Let the Divine Light always shine before me. Let not my knowledge fail me. I shall always say what is right and speak the truth.

After the "Om, Shanti, Shanti" had been uttered with the deepest reverence, Balkrishna began to sing. He sang the song of the true Vaishnava.

> He is the true Vaishnava who knows and feels another's woes as his own. Ever ready to serve, he never boasts. He bows to everyone and despises no one, keeping his thought, word and deed pure. Blessed is the mother of such an one. He reverences every woman as his mother. He keeps an equal mind and does not stain his lips with falsehood; nor does he touch another's wealth. No bonds of attachment can hold him. Ever in tune with Ramanama [the Divine King], his body possesses in itself all places of pilgrimage. Free from greed and deceit, passion and anger, this is the true Vaishnava.

It was strangely beautiful to think, almost aloud, as each of these passages was uttered, how appropriate they were; how the ideal had been so nearly reached, along the hard pathway of suffering, by the one who was lying there about to break his fast. Everyone felt their appropriateness and hearts were drawn together.

Before the actual breaking of the fast, Mahatma Gandhi turned to his friends. He spoke to them; and as he spoke his emotion was so deep that in his bodily weakness his voice could hardly be heard except by those who were nearest of all to him. He told them how for thirty years Hindu-Muslim unity had been his chief concern, and he had not yet succeeded in achieving it. He did not know what was the will of God, but on this day he would beseech them to promise to lay down their lives if necessary for the cause. The Hindus must be able to offer their worship with perfect freedom in their temples, and the Muslims be able to say their prayers with perfect freedom in their mosques. If this elementary freedom of worship could not everywhere be secured, then neither Hinduism nor Islam had any meaning.

Hakim Ajmal Khan and Maulana Abul Kalam Azad renewed their solemn pledge and promise on behalf of the Muslim community.

Then Dr. Ansari brought forward some orange juice and Mahatma Gandhi drank it. So the fast was broken. The joy and thankfulness of those who were present cannot adequately be described. Throughout it all, as congratulations poured in upon him, he lay there unmoved, quietly resting. Soon the room was left empty. Mahatma Gandhi remained in silence, and the great strain of breaking the fast was over.

¤   ¤   ¤

*At times of prayer or fasting, Gandhi often asked Andrews to sing for him the Christian hymns he loved best. These included: "When I Survey," "Lead, Kindly Light," and "Abide with Me." Of course he had his favorite Hindu hymns as well, and we read the opening verses of one of them in Andrews' account of the Great Fast: "The way of God is only meant for heroes . . . " The concluding verses of this hymn are worth recording too. They describe the hero's love for God.*

The pathway of love is the ordeal of fire
The shrinkers turn away from it.
Those who take the plunge into the fire attain
 eternal bliss.
Those who stand afar off, looking on, are scorched
 by the flames.
Love is a priceless thing, only to be won at the
 cost of death.
Those who live to die, these attain; for they have
 shed all thoughts of self.
Those heroic souls who are rapt in the love of the
Lord, they are the true lovers.

*Their common love for God, expressed in hymns like these, deepened the two friends' love for one another. The tenderness of their relations at this time, perhaps the time of closest communion in their lives, can be sensed from Andrews' side as he describes in a letter to Tagore how he would take his friend in his arms and carry him from his room to the sunny veranda, "just like a baby." Andrews had been faithful throughout the long vigil, although it had brought him to the edge of a nervous breakdown, as he confessed to Tagore. For his part, Gandhi wrote to Charlie, shortly after they parted in the month of October, to say: "I have missed you every moment today. Oh, your love!"*

*The fast itself resulted only in a pause in the rioting. Andrews records the great relief experienced all over India at the time of its end. Within two years, however, the rioting had broken out again and the Great Fast remained in memory only as a stirring symbol of what ought to be.*

# Chapter 9

## Untouchability

*I*n the pages of Young India *for December, 1927 Gandhi describes an encounter he and Andrews had with an untouchable in Orissa, a region where Andrews was well known because of his work in flood and famine relief. The narrative reminds us of an earlier incident in South Africa when the beaten indentured servant, Balasundaram, approached Gandhi for help. Here, too, the manifest humiliation of a single oppressed human being works like a burning glass to focus the reformer's energies on behalf of the masses. Gandhi entitled the account "Our Shame and Their Shame."*

¤     ¤     ¤

The long-deferred visit to Orissa has come to fill the bitter cup of sorrow and humiliation. It was at Bolgarh, thirty-one miles from the nearest railway station, that, whilst I was sitting and talking with Dinabandhu Andrews, a pariah with a half-bent back, wearing only a dirty loin-cloth, came crouching in front of us. He picked up a straw and put it in his mouth, and then lay flat on his face with arms outstretched. He then raised himself, folded his hands, bowed, took out the straw, arranged it in his hair, and was about to leave.

I was writhing in agony whilst I witnessed the scene. Immediately the performance was finished I called out for an interpreter, asked the friend to come near, and began to talk to him.

He was an "untouchable" living in a village six miles away, and, being in Bolgarh for the sale of his load of faggots and having heard of me, he had come to see me. When asked why he had taken the straw in his mouth, he said that this was to honour me. I hung my head in shame. The price of such "honour" seemed to me to be far too great to bear. My Hindu spirit was deeply wounded.

I asked him for a gift. He searched for a copper about his waist.

"I do not want your copper," I said to him in my misery.

"I want you to give me something better."

"I will give it," he replied.

I had ascertained from him that he drank liquor and ate carrion because it was the custom.

"The gift I want you to give me is a promise never again to take that straw in your mouth for any person on earth; it is beneath a man's dignity to do so; never again to drink, because it reduces man to the condition of a beast; never again to eat carrion, for it is against Hinduism, and no civilized person would ever eat carrion."

"But my people will excommunicate me if I do not eat carrion and drink," the poor man said.

"Then suffer the excommunication, and if need be leave the village."

The downtrodden, humble man made the promise. If he keeps it his threefold gift is more precious than all the rupees that generous countrymen entrust to my care.

This "untouchability" is our greatest shame. The humiliation of it is sinking deeper and deeper.

¤   ¤   ¤

*For Gandhi, untouchability stood like a great barrier before Indian independence.  He believed that Independence had to be freedom not only from foreign rule but from internal impurity as well.  "Swaraj is a meaningless term," he said, "if we desire to keep a fifth of India under perpetual subjection."*

*In Gandhi's eyes untouchability was a perversion of Hinduism.  He by no means rejected the caste system, understood as the traditional way of dividing people with respect to their callings.  What he did reject was any notion of "highness or lowness" attached to the four major castes, and he utterly opposed the continuation of a "fifth caste," made up of those who did society's dirty work and were considered to pollute others by their very touch.  The purification of Hinduism in this regard was so important to him that he doubted it could have a future otherwise.  "If we fail in this trial, Hinduism and Hindus will perish," he wrote in the pages of* Harijan, *his newspaper devoted to this cause.  Harijan means "children of God," the name Gandhi gave to those whom others called* Panchama *(fifth caste), or* Antyaja *(last born).*

*A major campaign for the rights of untouchables was planned by Gandhi during his period of recuperation at Juhu.  It centered on the town of* Vykom, *and became known as the* Vykom satyagraha. *The issue was the historic denial of the use of a main public road near the temple and the residences of the Brahmins. Muslims might use it, Christians, even dogs—but not untouchables.*

*Andrews was able to be in Vykom in 1925 to observe and describe this classic non-violent struggle.*

¤   ¤   ¤

A young Syrian Christian, a follower of Mr. Gandhi, who was by profession a barrister named George Joseph, had first determined to offer passive resistance against this inhuman prohibition. He took with him along the forbidden road an "untouchable." They were both beaten by the Brahmins for polluting the road. Then the police intervened. When George Joseph again made the attempt in company with a pariah he was arrested by the State police.

Immediately, in accordance with the plan of campaign, the whole company, who were with their leader, offered passive resistance in the same manner and were arrested also, until the State prisons were unable to bear the burden. Then the second phase in the struggle began. The police were instructed to make a cordon across the road. They were to allow only High-Caste people to pass, but to stop all "untouchables." Thereupon the passive resisters stood before the barrier in an attitude of prayer along with the "untouchables" day after day for many weeks. All the while the moral conscience of the Brahmins and of the State officials was being appealed to in various ways. The whole struggle was carried on without a single act of violence and in a deeply religious manner.

The crisis came when this part of the country became flooded with water during the monsoon. The water on the road reached as high as the waists of the passive resisters. The military police were allowed by the State to moor boats across the road, and to stand in them while on guard. The plight of the passive resisters became more and more pitiable; but they endured these hardships bravely and never gave way for a single hour.  In the end, after many months of such endurance, the State was able at last, with the consent of the Brahmins, to open the road.

¤   ¤   ¤

*Andrews was profoundly affected by the sheer human misery caused by untouchability in India, as he tells us in these personal accounts.*

¤   ¤   ¤

One day I was asked in Travancore by the "untouchables" themselves, through a messenger, whether I would be willing to meet them.  They had heard of me as Gandhi's brother, and they had sent this message to me.  When with joy I had accepted their invitation and had reached the place at midday, I found that more than three thousand of them had collected. Along with some devoted followers of Gandhi who were with me, we went up and down the rows of the "untouchables," encouraging them and showing our friendship.  It was necessary thus to go moving slowly through their midst until they had banished from their minds every last vestige of fear.  What I found out that day concerning the cruelty they received at the hands of the landlords, and the oppression from which they suffered, was a story of misery and wrong.  Their faces told me by their lines of suffering the truth of their tale.

. . . I can remember how, when I went near a poor untouchable woman in Malabar, who was crouching in her hut with three half-starved children by her side and with a mere skeleton of a baby in her arms, she screamed out in a terrible manner, even though I was wearing Indian home-spun clothes and could not possibly have been mistaken for an official.  She was possessed with the horrible fear that she might pollute me by her presence, and that I might in return perhaps do her some bodily injury.  The shock was to me so great when I saw her frightened face that it haunted me for many days.

¤　¤　¤

*Andrews never hesitated to prompt and encourage the Viceroy and political leaders in London to support Gandhi's initiatives on behalf of the untouchables.  Yet he knew that his role here must be marginal.  The important decisions had to be made by Hindus themselves, and success here hinged upon Gandhi.  Andrews was so aware of this that he even presumed upon their friendship by urging Gandhi to hold this one goal paramount in his work, fearing that his involvement in so many other political issues would pull Gandhi away from the* Harijan *cause.  A letter from Gandhi to Andrews in 1921 reveals Gandhi's sensitivity to such proddings from his friend, as well as the criticism he was receiving from Hindus who regarded him as too much under Andrews' Christian influence in a Hindu cause.  "I began this work," he writes, "before I ever heard of you."*

¤　¤　¤

You have inundated me with love-letters and I have neglected you.  But you have been ever in my thoughts and prayer.  You had no business to get ill.  You had therefore be better up and "doing."  And yet on your sick-bed you have been doing so much.  For I see more and more that praying is doing and that silence is the best speech and often the best argument.  And that is my answer to your anxiety about the untouchables.

I look at the problem as an Indian and a Hindu, you as an Englishman and a Christian.  You look at it with the eye of an observer, I as an affected and afflicted party.  You can be patient, and I cannot.  Or you as a disinterested reformer can afford to be impatient whereas I as a sinner must be patient if I would get rid of the sin.

. . . You are doing an injustice to me in even allowing yourself to think that for a single moment I may be subordinating the question to any other. But I need not give addresses or write in English upon it. Most of those who form my audience are not hostile to the "pariahs." I had the least difficulty about carrying the proposition about them in the Congress.

I began to think about you and the question at 2 a.m. Not being able to sleep I began to write to you at 4 a.m. I have not written all I want to say on the question. This is no apology. I have not been able to clear the point for you as it is clear to me. What you have written in your letter about students is right. You are thinking as an Englishman. I must not keep one thing from you. The *Gujarati* is endeavouring to weaken my proposition on the question by saying that I have been influenced by you in this matter, meaning thereby that I am not speaking as a Hindu but as one having been spoiled by being under your Christian influence. This is all rotten, I know. I began this work in South Africa before I ever heard of you and I was conscious of the sin of untouchability before I came under other Christian influences in South Africa.

The truth came to me when I was yet a child. I used to laugh at my dear mother for making us bathe if we brothers touched any pariah. It was in 1897 that I was prepared in Durban to turn Mrs. Gandhi away from the house because she would not treat on a footing of equality Lawrence, who she knew belonged to the pariah class and whom I had invited to stay with me. It has been a passion of my life to serve the untouchables because I have felt that I could not remain a Hindu if it was true that untouchability was a part of Hinduism.

. . . I may not finish the work in this incarnation. I shall be born again to finish that work or someone who has realized my agony will finish it. The point is, the Hindu way is different from the modern way. It is the way of *tapasya*. You will notice the use of the word "modern." For I do believe that the Christian way is not different from the Hindu. I am still not satisfied that I have told you all that is just now rising to my pencil. But I dare say I have said sufficient for you to understand. Only please do not take this letter to be a complaint if it is not to be taken as an apology.

¤   ¤   ¤

*Christian missionaries had made much of this moral failing of Hinduism, while converts to Christianity had been won from the ranks of the untouchables. Even though Christian practice was by no means perfect—Andrews was shocked to find Syrian Christians practicing untouchability within their church—Christian teaching about the worth and dignity of each individual soul served to expose the evil. Gandhi was aware of the effect of Christian influence here, yet he was quick to deny that his own convictions were based on Christian principles. He claimed that his opposition stemmed from childhood, and in this speech to a gathering of untouchables he tries to make that very clear.*

¤   ¤   ¤

I regard "untouchability" as the greatest blot on Hinduism. This idea was not brought home to me simply by my bitter experiences during the South African struggle. It is not, again, due to the fact that I was once an agnostic. It is equally wrong to think, as some people do, that I have taken my views from my study of Christian religious literature. These views of mine on this subject date as far back as the time when I was neither enamoured of, nor was acquainted with, the Bible or the followers of the Bible.

I was hardly yet twelve when this idea had dawned on me. A scavenger named Uka, an untouchable, used to attend our

139

house for cleaning latrines. Often I would ask my mother why it was wrong to touch him and why I was forbidden to do so. If I accidentally touched Uka, I was asked to perform the ablutions; and though I naturally obeyed, it was not without smilingly protesting that "untouchability" was not sanctioned by religion and that it was impossible that it should be so. I was a dutiful and obedient child; but so far as was consistent with respect for my parents I often had tussles with them on this matter. I told my mother that she was entirely wrong in considering physical contact with Uka as sinful; it could not be sinful.

While at school I would often happen to touch the "untouchables"; and, as I never would conceal the fact from my parents, my mother would tell me that the shortest cut to purification, after my unholy touch, was to cancel it by touching any Muslim passing by. Therefore simply out of reverence and regard for my mother I often did so, but never did so believing it to be a religious obligation.

. . . The fact that we addressed God as "the purifier of the polluted" shows that it is a sin to regard anyone born in Hinduism as polluted—that it is Satanic to do so. I have hence never tired of repeating that it is a great sin. I do not pretend that this thing had crystallized as a conviction in me at the age of twelve, but I do say that I did then regard "untouchability" as a sin.

There was a time when I was wavering between Hinduism and Christianity. When I recovered my balance of mind I felt that to me salvation was possible only through the Hindu religion, and my faith in Hinduism grew deeper and more enlightened. But even then I believed that "untouchability" was not for me.

So long as Hindus willfully regard "untouchability" as part of their religion, so long as the mass of Hindus consider it a sin to touch a section of their brethren, *swaraj* is impossible of attainment.

But I have faith in me still. I have realized that the spirit of kindness whereof the poet Tulsidas sings so eloquently, which forms the corner-stone of the Jain and Vaishnava religions, which is the quintessence of the *Bhagavata* and behind every verse in the *Gita*—this kindness, this love, this charity is slowly but steadily gaining ground in the hearts of the masses of this country.

I was at Nellore on National Day. I met the "untouchables" there, and I prayed as I have done today. I *do* want to attain spiritual deliverance. I do not want to be reborn. But if I have to be reborn I should wish to be born an "untouchable" so that I may share their sorrows, sufferings, and the affronts levelled at them, in order that I may endeavor to free myself and them from that miserable condition. Therefore I prayed that if I should be born again I should be so, not as a Brahmin, Kshattriya, Vaishya, or Shudra, but as an "untouchable."

¤ ¤ ¤

*In his own way, Andrews expressed empathy with the outcasts and tried to call forth the same response from others. In a sermon preached all over the south of India in 1922, Andrews appeals to the adherents of all the great world religions to respond to the plight of the untouchables. His text is Matthew 15:32, "I have compassion on the multitude."*

¤ ¤ ¤

I saw only three days ago a sight which filled my heart with sadness. We went out to a village in the Madras Presidency and there was to be a welcome to the great poet [Tagore], and I went a little before the poet, and there in the village there were villagers and others with all preparations to meet the

141

poet, and then in another place away from them were some wretched poverty-stricken half-naked men, women, and little children, and I said, "Who are these?" They said, "These are *Panchamas*." I went to love them and they ran away. They actually began to run away in fear of me, and it broke my heart to see the fear towards me. And then I told one of them to tell them not to run away but to come nearer, and I went to them with love and embraced them, and though I could not speak to them in words they knew I loved them in my heart. They were kept away in the background. They had no place in the welcome of the poet. And then someone at a distance asked them by a sign to prostrate themselves, and they fell down and rubbed their foreheads in the dust. That was the sight that filled my heart with pity.

There is only one thing I want to say and that is this—"I have compassion on the multitude." That is what Christ said. That is what Buddha said before. It is a very simple word. It needs a tender heart. Is there not someone in this church who could take this up, live among them, live the whole of their lives among them? Be a *Panchama*, feel their sufferings and touch them. If I could see my way to give up other duties, how I wish I could do it. Why cannot some of you do that? I ask you as human beings, not as Hindus, not as Christians, not as Mahomedans, but as men who are human beings, cannot you remove the burden?

¤   ¤   ¤

*When Andrews wrote about untouchability in* Mahatma Gandhi's Ideas, *he took the title of the essay with which this chapter begins and applied it to the Christian church. The phrase "our shame and their shame" had become for him emblematic of untouchability in Hinduism and racism in Christianity. Racism was Christianity's parallel evil—he felt he must devote his energy to it just as Gandhi devoted himself to the banishing of untouchability.*

*In 1932, when Gandhi was risking his life by fasting on behalf of untouchables, Andrews wrote to him in order to define his own personal goal in these terms: "Wherever I go, this must be the conscious object—to deal a blow at untouchability within the Christian Church. You have brought me back, with a shock, to the one purpose for which God gave me life and health and strength. I thank God for that."*

*During the same year, in an address to Christian ministers in England, Andrews said he longed for the day "when untouchability shall be removed, not only in India, but in South Africa, the southern states of America, and everywhere where Christians refuse to worship with their brethren whose complexion is slightly darker than their own."*

*We should not forget that Andrews' deepest commitment throughout his life was the ending of racial inequality in whatever form it took. "That is reality, that is truth for me," he wrote to Gandhi. A revealing statement occurs in a letter to Horace Alexander in 1929. Andrews was visiting the United States and had just attended a discussion at Yale University about race relations studies in American universities. "When Gandhi asks for a change of heart," he writes to Alexander, "it is really a changed racial outlook which he requires."*

*This commitment to racial equality shaped Andrews' political commitment. When he argued for complete independence for India, it was because he believed anything short of that could only fail; the idea of white supremacy had too strong a hold on the European mind. His criticism of organized religion had to do with the church's practice of racial exclusion. Theologically speaking, it was the unity*

*of humankind, including all races and outcast peoples,
which was for Andrews "the fundamental principle for
which Christ died upon the cross."*

*His desire to center his whole life upon this principle was
so strong that it inevitably colored his advice to Gandhi as
well; hence Andrews repeatedly urged Gandhi to give first
priority to the question of untouchability. It was unrealistic
on his part to expect Gandhi to become a "single-issue"
leader, yet when Andrews asked him to do just that, as in
this letter of 1933, we can sense the tremendous importance of this issue for them both.*

¤   ¤   ¤

Haven't you been trying to serve two masters, and if you
have given your life as a hostage for "untouchability removal,"
does not that mean entire concentration on that issue for the
whole remainder of your life without turning to the right or to
the left?

I want to work that out and "think aloud," as you rightly put
it. You staked your life itself on this one issue—removal of this
curse. Can you now go and use that life in other secondary
issues? I want you to answer that question. I am quite unworthy
even to put it, because I haven't risked my life at all and am
living here in comparative ease. . . .

You may say—and it may be right—that without Purna
*Swaraj* [complete independence] you will always be blocked
on this very question by some obstruction from an alien
government. I can understand that argument. . . . But there is
another moral argument that you have used again and again.
It is this: "We are not fit to attain *Purna Swaraj* while we go
on treating our *Harijan* brothers and sisters like this." You have
all the moral force behind you if you are led to take this
course—to say to the world, "My life is now entirely a hostage
for the *Harijans*."

# Chapter 10

## Interpreting Gandhi

Andrews was a constant traveler. He would sing of himself, mocking both his poverty and his globe-trotting ways: "A wandering Christian I, a thing of shreds and patches." And wherever he went—South Africa, Kenya, British Guiana, Canada or the United States—he was known as the friend and interpreter of Gandhi. Culturally, Andrews was able to bridge the gap between East and West; as he wrote in a letter from America to Horace Alexander, "in a very wonderful way the American people have come to like me both as an Englishman and as an Indian, if I may dare to say so." Politically Andrews was very effective in translating Gandhi's goals and methods in ways that could be understood and supported outside of India.

Between 1929 and 1931 he published three books about Gandhi which were widely read in England and the United States. He expressed his hopes for the first of the trilogy, Mahatma Gandhi's Ideas, in a letter to Gandhi in 1928.

¤    ¤    ¤

I am more anxious than I can tell you that this book which I am writing may really be informing and inspiring, and may also be sufficiently lucid and popular to be read by average people, both in Europe and America . . . I really do think, if I might dare in deepest humility to say so, that this year, in which I have been in England and Europe, and the coming visit to America, will both do something to prepare the way for the time when you do actually come.

¤    ¤    ¤

*Gandhi would not actually come to England until the fall of 1931, but the preparation for his visit and the interpretation of his work were of critical importance, especially as the Indian campaign for independence was renewed in earnest in 1930.*

*In 1928, six years after the suspension of civil disobedience following the massacre of policemen at Chauri Chaura, Gandhi had signaled the resumption of* satyagraha *on a limited scale. In 1929 he was once again lighting bonfires of imported foreign cloth. Meanwhile, efforts to advance towards dominion status for India within the Empire had met resistance in the British Parliament, where the new prime minister, Ramsay MacDonald, could not command a majority.*

*Thus emboldened by the renewed popular movement and frustrated by the slowness of the British response, on New Year's Day of 1930 the Indian National Congress declared that "swaraj is now to mean complete independence." Widespread disobedience was now sanctioned, its shape and form to be determined by Gandhi. While he waited for the "inner voice" to direct his actions, Gandhi heard from Andrews, "I cannot tell you how much I have been thinking of you! At such times as these I have realised that thoughts are prayers. The greatest of all struggles has* begun and India is right, as I have always believed, in claiming nothing short of independence."

During the spring of 1930 Gandhi began his most decisive satyagraha, the great Salt March to Dandi on the seacoast, where he would pick up some salt from the shore and thus defying the British monopoly of this element essential for life. The march involved thousands of protesters, while subsequent expanded actions involving possession of salt resulted in the jailings of perhaps 100,000 people. Non-violent discipline was maintained; the organizers had learned the lesson of Chauri Chaura. One of Gandhi's biographers, Louis Fischer, judges the result of this campaign as making "England powerless and India invincible."

The immediate result for Gandhi was reimprisonment in Yeravda Prison. From there he corresponded with his many friends, including Andrews, although there were also times when it seemed he relied on a kind of mental telepathy. Gandhi said once to a follower, when he had decided not to write to Charlie: "I would far rather let my silence speak to him. The pen is often a superfluity, if not a hindrance, to the heart's flow."

Andrews himself did not hesitate to write and cable frequently as he engaged in an effort to convince both the Viceroy, Lord Irwin, and Gandhi to reach a settlement. When the Gandhi-Irwin Pact was signed Andrews rejoiced, for the way was now clear for Gandhi to come to England as the representative of Congress at the Second Round Table Conference.

These round table conferences were a means used by the British Labor Government to bring together representatives of India's various constituencies and leaders of Britain's three political parties to consider proposals for India's future. The first conference had been boycotted by Congress, but now Gandhi, freed from prison, would attend. Andrews went to work at Whitehall and Downing Street in order to prepare the way for him.

Agatha Harrison, a spirited woman who had stepped forward at this time to serve as Andrews' personal secretary and would devote years of her life to the Indian cause, remembered one sentence about Gandhi constantly recurring in the letters Andrews sent to British officials: "I can only tell you that after nearly 20 years experience I have never known in my life a more essentially truthful man, even in the smallest of details. If you are to deal with him at all, it will be necessary for you to share that belief with me, and I can see clearly how difficult such a faith will be to you—yet nothing can be done without it. On no other basis except this confidence in Mr. Gandhi's honesty and sincerity can the situation in India come to a right settlement."

Andrews' other great concern was for Gandhi's relationship with the unemployed mill workers of Lancashire. Gandhi's boycott of English-made cloth was taking jobs away from these workers at a time when they were already hard-hit because of the worldwide economic depression. Andrews went so far as to ask Gandhi to call off the boycott of foreign cloth before coming to England. He wrote to Gandhi describing the suffering he had seen for himself in Lancashire. Gandhi replied: "As is your wont, you are distressed over what your eyes see and your ears hear. This time it is the terrible unemployment in Lancashire. What you see and hear acts as an effective barrier against perceiving the truth. I have always found it true that hard cases make bad law! The way you suggest is not the way to help Lancashire."

Yet he promised Charlie that he would visit the workers in Lancashire; and when he did, with Andrews as his guide, *they received him with great warmth and affection. "I am one of the unemployed," an English worker said, "but if I was in India I would say the same thing that Mr. Gandhi is saying."*

*Andrews arranged for rooms for Gandhi and his party at 88 Knightsbridge in London. Gandhi was displeased. He had wanted to take humble quarters in a poor part of the city; but Andrews insisted that the demands of the conference justified this more central, more expensive location. Once installed there, Andrews took up the role of doorkeeper he had played before, in Delhi in 1924. At Knightsbridge, Horace Alexander was like a member of the family; and it was in that very crowded and busy place that he remembers their mutual laughter.*

*Gandhi captured the imagination of the British, not least by his sense of humor. At tea with King George V and Queen Mary he was dressed in loincloth, sandals, shawl, and his large dangling watch. Later, someone asked him if he had had enough on. "The King," he replied, "had enough on for both of us."*

*The conference itself, however, was not productive. It became a clamor of conflicting interests, as Moslems, Sikhs, Christians, untouchables, princes and planters sought to safeguard their positions. Andrews described the conference as "a magnificent failure," acknowledging that no progress towards Indian independence had been made. In fact, when Gandhi returned to India in January, 1932, it was only a matter of weeks before he was arrested and imprisoned again, and Congress was proscribed.*

*Meanwhile, Andrews had gone to South Africa to help prepare for a round table conference there between Indian and South African leaders. But when he heard of Gandhi's arrest, he set sail for India immediately. Upon his arrival in mid-March, he found that the military had been repress-*

*ing the independence movement with great severity. Some 30,000 people had been arrested during civil disobedience campaigns. "It is like 1919 in the Punjab," he wrote in a warning letter to British authorities. He was not allowed to visit Gandhi in jail, and had to deal with the despair of that time solely from his own spiritual resources. We have a poignant account of Andrews' sufferings at that time from some passages in* Christ in the Silence, *written the following year.*

¤   ¤   ¤

Last year, at this season of Easter, I was at Delhi, in India; and I spent Good Friday there also under the shadow of the cross. A gloom was over all the land. Wherever I went, from one Indian home to another, the sense of impotence was mingled with despair. Hopelessness seemed to be settling down on the face of the earth.

In my own life also the shadows had deepened. The season itself was the beginning of the heat. There was the parched dry atmosphere of the dusty plains. The monsoon rains were still far off. Nature herself seemed to speak of decay and death.

The chaplain of St. James's Church had asked me to give a message in church on Easter Sunday evening, and I found it extremely difficult beforehand to raise my thoughts above the depressing atmosphere around me. Such was the gloom of failure and disappointment that I hardly knew what to say or how to speak.

Then before the Easter communion in the early morning, in the cool of the day, as I sat in the silence of the church, the oppression which had been so heavy upon me was suddenly relieved. For I read over before the service the story of Mary in the garden as she meets her risen Lord. The marvellous beauty of the scene—the dimness of the early dawn, the sheltered garden, Mary's first thought that He was the gardener, the one word "Mary," the immediate recognition, "Rabboni, my Master!" Surely never was there a more beautiful story told than this! As I read the words and pictured the scene I found the weight upon my mind, which I had felt all through the week, wonderfully lifted; and I could almost see His form as Mary touched his feet in love and worship. Her tears were turned into joy as she knew that her Lord was not taken away but was with her, by her side.

Even as her tears were turned into joy, so also my own heart was lightened and the gladness of the realisation of Christ's presence came back to me in full measure in the Easter dawn. For I could now say, in the midst of all the clouds of darkness enveloping India, "Christ is risen! Christ is risen!" His new and endless life would be given in full measure to the Indian people whom I loved.

¤   ¤   ¤

*The energy that Andrews received through this Easter encounter with Christ was poured into a round of meetings with governmental officials in England, where he returned in May of 1932. He argued strongly against the policy of repression in India and attempted to restore the confidence of Prime Minister Ramsay MacDonald in Gandhi's intentions.*

*There were many lectures and public meetings. The publication at this time of* What I Owe to Christ *caused many to listen respectfully to what Andrews had to say when he spoke about the moral imperative before England with regard to India. His relations with the Church of England were also on the mend, for the church began to regard him now as more of an asset than a threat. He was a prophet who was beginning to receive some honor in his own country. The one who knew the prophet best was Agatha*

*Harrison, and she provides us with this very human portrait.*

◘    ◘    ◘

It is a great experience to work with him. To do so successfully one must believe very thoroughly in the kind of thing this man does. And it certainly has its humorous side. For instance, he may be one or even two hours late for an appointment; or, you expect him back from London at a certain time, plan important interviews accordingly—and receive a wire to say he is not coming. You await his arrival prepared to point out all the inconvenience the delay has caused, but find you do not voice it, for he has a sense of the relative importance of things, which if you do not always agree with, you must respect. In truth, he is a prophet, and to such a great deal is forgiven.

He never keeps a diary. A thoughtful hostess provided him with a beautiful blue leather one specially suited for a man's pocket. All his engagements she had carefully written in as far as she knew them. When he was turning out his papers preparatory to going to Africa, this unused diary was among them—it had never been used. I wonder how many people have tried to alter this man's habits, and failed!

He has no home, yet has any man or woman so many homes? For to whatever part of the world he may go there are ever open doors. He shares what he has and expects other people to do the same.

No wonder that he radiates happiness, for he has the love and trust of such a variety of people. What an experience it is to walk with him down Gower Street in London, where the Indian student hostel is situated! Faces light up. I remember in particular one day when we were doing this. The papers that morning had been full of the news of the resignation of the "moderates," as a result of the statement of the secretary of state for India. All the papers mirrored the depth of misunderstanding and bitterness between this country and India. Yet suddenly there came towards us two Indian men, one of whom rushed to C. F. Andrews as though he had seen a light, and touched his feet in reverence.

What will be his next move? Who can tell? For people who walk so closely with God have to be ready to obey His behest. He will be in this country probably until October, working on the challenge that the Indian situation presents to the Christian and peace forces. After that I seem to see two shabby suit cases being packed with a most curious medley of clothes, unanswered letters, chapters of a new book, unfinished articles, and this "echo" will be off to some other part of the world "to break its sleep of habit or despair."

◻ ◻ ◻

*Andrews' work in England greatly intensified in September, 1932, when Gandhi announced from prison a "fast unto death" on behalf of the untouchables. At issue was Britain's decision to establish a separate electorate for the "depressed classes." Such a separation, Gandhi believed, would disrupt Hindu society by permanently stigmatizing the untouchables. To Ramsay MacDonald he wrote: "I have to resist your decision with my life. The only way I can do it is by declaring a perpetual fast unto death from food of any kind save water with or without salt and soda." He set the date of September 20 to begin.*

*"The Epic Fast," as it came to be known, lasted only until the afternoon of September 26, but it very nearly cost Gandhi's life. The whole of India responded, realizing the choice he had put before them, a choice that transcended the immediate question of the electorates. Were they willing to maintain untouchability at the price of the Mahatma's own life? After the fast, even though old habits*

and practices were often maintained, untouchability had lost its public sanction.

In order to save Gandhi's life, agreement had to be reached in India among representatives of the untouchables and various political factions. When that was achieved in the Yeravda Pact, England then had to accept the new electoral arrangements and do so with great promptness, for Gandhi was sinking every day. Andrews' biographers credit the intensity of his "planned, sustained and concentrated work" with making this possible.

Andrews had wanted to be at Gandhi's side during the fast and pleaded with him to postpone it until he could come. Gandhi cabled his response: "Regard fasting God's call. Only certain prospect of withdrawal separate electorate for depressed can warrant postponement. In my opinion your presence more useful there." Indeed it was, since Andrews had access to the prime minister and could play again the part he had played in Pretoria in 1914.

Interpreting the "Epic Fast" to the West was not easy. The English were puzzled by such an extreme act. Tagore wondered if they failed to understand because they could not comprehend the way of non-violence at all. He noted that the English had been more than ready to kill and be killed in order to prevent the dismemberment of the United Kingdom when Ireland sought to separate itself from British rule; yet they could not appreciate this offering of a single life to prevent the permanent division of Indian society.

The fast presented a problem, however, even to those in the West who understood non-violence. Was not a fast until death an act of violence itself? Andrews struggled with this question. In an essay for the Christian Century in October, 1932, called "Gandhi Offers His Life," he justified *the action because of Gandhi's burning love for the* harijans *and tried to see it through the lens of the Gospel of John.*

◻    ◻    ◻

But what are we to say concerning such moral compulsion? Is it truly an ethical mode of procedure? Can such a fast be justified? Is it not, after all, a form of violence in disguise? Is there really any difference between this moral violence and certain acts of physical violence which Mahatma Gandhi himself deplores?

It is true, there is a violence about it. I think Mahatma Gandhi would himself acknowledge this. But he would call it the compulsion of love, and he would say that only under the compulsion of extreme and intense love can such acts of moral violence be performed without departing from the law of *satyagraha*, or soul-force. On a previous occasion, when he "fasted unto death" against the mill-owners of Ahmedabad, he acknowledged that this fast of his was not free from a "grave defect." For he had enjoyed very close and cordial relations with the mill-owners, and his fast could not but modify their decision [in the strike situation]. He then wrote as follows: "With the mill-owners I could only plead. To fast against them would amount to coercion. Yet, in spite of my knowledge that my fast was bound to coerce, as in fact it did, I felt I could not help it. The duty to undertake it seemed to me to be clear."

Here the intensity of his love was for the poor, downtrodden mill-hands; he was ready to go to the extremest lengths which love could urge in fighting their great battle; and he won. With the untouchables, his love is far deeper still. Indeed, it may be said to be the deepest thing in all his life. He loves them with a love that is stronger than death itself. Therefore he has felt justified in employing the same desperate moral compulsion, a fast unto death, in order to help them at this critical juncture.

He saw the poorest of poor people, whom he loved so deeply, taking a wrong turn, which led to a hidden precipice. With all the reckless daring of devoted love he threw himself across their path. Even if his own life must be lost, with untold agonies in the process, he would sacrifice it for their sake.

Surely in such a deed there is a beauty, rare and wonderful, which brings back to mind the words, "Greater love hath no man than this, that a man lay down his life for his friends."

¤ ¤ ¤

*In November of 1932, Gandhi announced his intention once again to fast until death. The fast would begin on January 1, 1933, in support of the right of untouchables to enter temples in India. This time, however, Andrews was personally very troubled. From England, where he was continuing his work with Horace Alexander, Agatha Harrison, and other members of the India Conciliation Group, he wrote to Gandhi and poured out his concerns.*

¤ ¤ ¤

The whole of my religious upbringing has been such as to make any thought of suicide on my part impossible.

I am really troubled still. Such a practice as this, if it is not uniquely used for a God-given opportunity, will certainly be used by fanatics to force an issue which may be reactionary instead of progressive. Human madness or even doting affection may become tyrannical in this way. How far my anxieties and fears are mixed with weak human affection I can hardly myself understand. I *do* know that I saw you finally giving your life itself for the depressed classes, in your last fast, and I was glad—I saw in it the "greater love." I can see you now preparing to do the same thing on January 1st, if the temple authorities do not give way.

It seems to me that I would very gladly lay down my life to remove "untouchability" between the white race fanatics who call themselves Christians and the other races. But you have evidently come to the point of *forcing the issue*—literally *forcing* it, and I have to think that out in terms of Christ.

I think He *did* force the issue, when He set His face steadfastly to go to Jerusalem. He saw then, I think, that only His own death could call the Jewish leaders to a halt. There is one strange saying of His, "The Kingdom of Heaven suffereth violence, and the violent take it by force." Again I am not sure whether His act in cleansing the temple was not of the same character, i.e., forcing the issue. But the method of fasting, committing suicide, still instinctively repels me.

¤   ¤   ¤

*In an earlier exchange on this subject, Gandhi had written to Charlie in a humorous vein, "I assure you I do not want to kill brother ass [St. Francis's term for the body]. He is in God's safekeeping. If He means to starve him, neither your effort nor mine can save him. For the present he is flourishing on goat's milk and plenty of fruit with some homemade bread thrown in."*

*In response to this letter from Andrews, Gandhi simply repeats his appeal to the will of God. He does not engage Andrews' perplexities directly. Perhaps the two cables from Andrews he alludes to had shown a greater understanding and support for the fast.*

¤   ¤   ¤

December 20, 1932

My Dear Charlie,

I have your letter posted days after it was written, and I have your two dear cables. I was wondering whether the later developments in the anti-untouchability campaign, including the prospective fast, were thoroughly understood by you. Your wires show that you have understood them fully, and I am so glad, for, whereas the fast in connection with the British decision was appreciated by many, the one contemplated to take place on the 2nd January next is misunderstood by many, and I am afraid that you might not understand it at all, whereas to me the necessity is clearer than when I fasted about the British decision.

The British decision was a political issue, though with me it had a deeply religious significance. In the present instance, it is a purely religious issue. I have given many explanations in defence of it. All of them put together fall far short of what I feel about it, but what, I have no adequate language to express. Of course, for me personally, it transcends reason, because I feel it to be a clear call from God. My position is that there is nothing just now that I am doing of my own accord. He guides me from moment to moment.

This is a thing which you cannot make other people believe, and it would be quite proper for them to reject such testimony. That has happened before now. That which was claimed as the voice of God proved to be the prompting of the Devil. What it is in my case will be partly judged by results and partly after my death, never wholly in any case and at any time except by God. After all, the intention behind an act is the final criterion, and that God alone can know, not even the author of the intention. I hope that you got my cable already in answer to yours from Birmingham.

I am quite clear that your presence is most useful there, and you are not to have anxiety complex if I have to fast. You at least will have no difficulty in believing that if I enter upon the fast, it would be by God's will, and He will keep me intact if He has more service to take through this body,

With love and greetings from all of us . . .

Mohan

◻ ◻ ◻

*Andrews worked diligently in London for legislation that would open the Hindu temples to the untouchables, and the prospect of such legislation finally led Gandhi to postpone the fast. When he wrote to Andrews about this decision, he was ministering once more to his friend's anxiety on his behalf.*

◻ ◻ ◻

January 6, 1933

My dear Charlie,

I have your letters. I am quite sure that your work still lies there for some time at least, and when I feel otherwise there will be no hesitation in sending an S.O.S. If you could but get a month's quiet at Woodbrooke, there will be some rest for your nerves. I can well understand what the constant rush amid all the din and noise of railway traffic must mean to you. I hope you will have the needed time to finish your book on "The Sermon on the Mount."

I have your two cables telling me that you were working in connection with [the temple entry bill]. Anyway till at least the fate is known, the fast stands postponed. I am hoping that you have ceased to worry about it. There can be no anxiety about anything that comes from God. Did I ever give you the rendering of a verse we have every day at the morning prayer? "Adversity is no adversity, nor is prosperity real prosperity. Real adversity consists in forgetting God's omnipresence, and real prosperity consists in its constant remembrance." If then the fast comes from God, where is there the slightest cause for anxiety? . . .

With love from us all,
Mohan

◻   ◻   ◻

*In a letter to a close adviser to Prime Minister Mac-Donald, written that same month, Andrews made a strong case for the temple entry legislation, going so far as to estimate the political damage that would result should Gandhi indeed carry out a fast to the death.*

◻   ◻   ◻

You have to consider carefully the extreme risks involved in keeping Mr. Gandhi in prison in this way. You are not dealing with an educated community, but one in which legend takes the place of fact. If for any reason, Mahatma Gandhi dies in gaol, he will be a legend for hundreds of years to come, and the power which imprisoned him will undoubtedly be regarded as the cause of his death by popular legendary opinion. Is it worthwhile running the risk, when he has already declared that he is giving the rest of his life as a hostage to the untouchables?

◻   ◻   ◻

*In May of 1933, even though progress had been achieved on issues related to untouchability, Gandhi believed himself led by God to undertake a twenty-one day fast of "purification for service." Because this was a fast of specified duration, and not "unto death," Andrews felt freer to respond positively, though many others were simply bewildered by the act. He cabled Gandhi:* ACCEPT YOUR DECISION AND UNDERSTAND. LOVE, CHARLIE.

*Gandhi replied: "I treasure the telegram you sent me. I was thankful to God that you had understood."*

*A cable message every day of the fast, sent from Woodbrooke, outside Birmingham, where he was staying with the Quakers, would be Andrews' way of standing with his friend on this occasion. His intercession with the authorities had also been instrumental in securing Gandhi's early release from prison—in time for the fast to begin on May 18th.*

*Before the year 1933 was out, however, Gandhi was back in Yeravda Prison, sentenced to a one-year term for his renewed civil disobedience activities. This time he was refused permission to work on his newspaper,* Harijan, *while imprisoned.*

*In response to this restriction on his work, Gandhi began another fast, which he described as being "for my consolation." Andrews went to India, against Gandhi's advice, hoping to dissuade him from fasting. For the effect of this fast on Gandhi's body was devastating and he had to be hospitalized. Although unable to prevent it, Andrews played a crucial, even life-saving role when he finally reached Gandhi and helped bring the fast to an end. In this letter to Horace Alexander he describes the scene and tells him how he persuaded Gandhi to live.*

¤     ¤     ¤

On Wednesday, the danger zone was reached. When I saw him at 11:30 a.m. he could only speak with difficulty . . . He had distributed his little things as last bequests. My own visit rallied him, and I made him promise he would fight for life and [said] that if I felt the last word had been said by the Government, I would be the first to tell him and let him die in peace; but I did not believe it. I got him to promise to continue to struggle for life and take water. Then I hurried to the Home Secretary, but I found that the doctor had already warned him. Just as I began to tell the Home Secretary what I had seen personally, the doctor came back and very soon after that the release order was signed.

Fortunately there was no one about when the doctor and I went through the passages to tell him he was released. We both pressed him to take his orange juice before the ambulance came, and I said Sanskrit prayers and sang his favorite hymns, "Lead, Kindly Light" and "When I Survey." Dr. Cama came to say goodbye. He raised his head with great difficulty and said: "Thank you, Doctor, for your exquisite kindness!"

¤     ¤     ¤

*What can we make of these differences between the two friends concerning fasting? Certainly, as this last episode reveals, it was Charlie's concern to preserve the life and health of his friend that was at the root of any difference. But we also see here a continuation of the argument about the moral purity of the non-violent witness. We think of Andrews' earlier criticisms of Gandhi's army recruitment activities as well as his burning of foreign cloth.*

*Andrews confessed that there were times when the moral compulsion and extreme self-sacrifice of such fasts were called for—but how many times? Do we not see two different valuations being placed on human existence: one Christian, one Hindu? For Gandhi, after all, this existence was not the only one. He once wrote Andrews that if he did not finish his work in this existence he would be born again to finish it.*

*The two men differed in their valuation of the body as well. Andrews never condoned any extreme of asceticism. He could neither understand nor support Gandhi's rule of celibacy—within marriage. Single and celibate as he was himself, he insisted on affirming the body as God's good gift. Gandhi, however, was able to write to Andrews that all that kept him in the flesh was his work to emancipate the untouchables. To depart the flesh by means of a fast for that very cause would be an act of integrity.*

*Gandhi wrote about his views on fasting to many of his friends, for it was not only Andrews who had difficulty understanding these acts. To one follower he explained that fasting should be seen as a form of* tapascharya, *or ascetic self-discipline. "Whenever a religion had lost its vitality, men of sincere devotion went through extreme* tapascharya *to restore life to it. Without such* tapascharya, *no religious awakening can be brought about."*

*In a letter to another follower, written on December 23, 1932, he asked: "Why do you think that my fast was due to disappointment? On the contrary, it sprang from hope eternal. Fasting is as necessary for life as eating. It is a necessary part of prayer. We serve as well by dying as by living. But it is the privilege of the few to have to fast. Needless to say, I write of spiritual fasts. I know that fasting may come also from despair. Then it is rank suicide. I should defend my fast against such a charge. For me it has always been a process of penance and purification. . . . The basis of all penitential fasts has always been faith in mankind, God, and oneself. It gives an inward joy that sustains one. I therefore want you to share with me the joy of it."*

*On this matter of penance one would expect Andrews and Gandhi to see eye to eye, yet there are clearly differences even here, as these lines in a letter from Andrews to a coworker reveal. At times Andrews responded to Gandhi like any other Englishman; had he not, he could hardly have played his valuable role as interpreter.*

¤  ¤  ¤

He feels that the suffering of his fast is needed to purge the atmosphere. When I said to him, "I can see that you as a Hindu have a different idea of the spiritual effect of suffering from us," he said at once: "Yes, that is so. And it came clear to me in reading your new book, *Christ in the Silence.* You are very 'English' in that, but also you are Indian. I can see two strains in you. I want to interpret the English side. I can see that I am antagonising them, and it is the last thing I want to do—I want to win them."

# Chapter 11

## Religious Truth

*G*andhi *was often approached by Christian missionaries and questioned by them about the proper relationship between Hinduism and Christianity. They were concerned somehow to uphold the integrity of the missionary calling before a man whom it might seem presumptuous to attempt to convert. When Gandhi responded to their questions he would present Charlie Andrews as the example to follow for any Christian missionary who truly wished to serve God and the people of India. When asked in one such group session what he thought was the right way of "giving the Good News," Gandhi responded this way.*

¤   ¤   ¤

I suggest that God did not bear the cross only 1900 years ago, but He bears it today. It would be poor comfort to the world if it had to depend upon a historical God who died 2,000 years ago. Do not then preach the God of history, but show

Him as He lives today through you.  In South Africa I met a number of [Christian] friends, and read a number of books— Pearson, Parker and Butler—all giving their own interpretations, and I said to myself, I must not bother myself with these conflicting interpretations.  It is better to allow our lives to speak for us than our words.  C. F. Andrews never preaches.  He is incessantly doing his work.  He finds enough work and stays where he finds it and takes no credit for bearing the cross.  I have the honour to know hundreds of honest Christians, but I have not known one better than Andrews.

¤　¤　¤

*In this chapter we will see how Gandhi and Charlie Andrews viewed their religious convictions, particularly the relationship between Christianity and Hinduism, and how they each dealt with the difficult question of conversion from one faith to another.  Their own life experiences were such that each could bring a fresh angle of vision to these questions of religious truth.  Gandhi had been strongly influenced by Christianity but never converted, while Andrews' point of view was that of a Christian missionary whose methods seemed to leave little room for traditional evangelization, but constantly bore witness to his faith in Christ.*

*Andrews often reflected upon his encounter as a Christian with India and Indian philosophy.  We should remember that he had been well prepared by his studies with Bishop Westcott at Cambridge and had, in fact, come to India seeking a more profound understanding of Christ.*

¤　¤　¤

I have often been asked:  What difference has the change of environment from England to India made in your outlook upon religion?  Are you conscious of a new perspective?  Has the centre of gravity shifted? The first change I have to relate is the expansion of all my previous ideas with regard to Christ's work and presence in all the world, and of what is meant by the word Christian. I recall to mind almost daily the freedom with which Christ himself accepted the faith of the Roman centurion, the Samaritan woman, the Greeks who came to him, and again the Syro-Phoenician woman. The orthodox among his contemporaries would have excluded them from the fold of the faithful, but not Christ himself. No outward profession had any value for him apart from the faith that went with it. Hypocrisy was felt by him to be one of the most deadly sins.

I have met in India, on a very extensive scale, those whom I could recognize at once to be far above me in simplicity and self-denial, in humility and thirst for God. I cannot for a moment think of these persons as alien to Christ's teaching. In the East I have found Christ far beyond the narrow limitations of sect and creed, and it became absurd to divide mankind into compartments which are only misleading. The poet Tennyson has sung:

Our little systems have their day,

They have their day and cease to be.

They are but broken lights of Thee,

And Thou, O Lord, art more than they.

It was necessary for me to let go the "little system" which had confined me before, as though it was the final expression of the Christian faith. The words of St. John, written in his extreme old age, are universal in their scope and range: "Beloved, let us love one another, for love is of God, and everyone that loves is born of God and knows God." Here there is no limitation. Love wherever found is of God, for God is love. Somehow it took me a strangely long time to break through all limitations and to recognize goodness everywhere as the mark of the working of God in human life.

When we turn from the lives of Indian people to their sacred scriptures, we find passages of deep spiritual beauty and moral insight. I take for an example one famous passage from the *Dammapada*: "Let a man overcome anger by love, let him overcome evil by good: let him overcome greed by liberality, and the liar by truth." Here is the very sentiment of the Sermon on the Mount expressed in the noblest form. Again, it would be difficult to find anything more "Christian" in spirit than the following passage from the *Granth Saheb*: "Farid, if a man beat thee, beat him not in return, but kiss his feet."

With such passages as these before me, and lives which correspond to the teaching, it has very greatly helped me to turn to a writer such as Clement of Alexandria and to note how the early Christian thinkers emancipated themselves from the narrower conceptions of God. . . . Christ, they taught, was the universal Son of Man, not only the "Son of David"; he was the light that lightens every man that comes into the world. It was impossible for me to doubt that these Greek Fathers, if they had come face to face with higher Indian religious thought, would have sought to embrace, within the universal conception of Christian, those gifts and graces which Hinduism has to offer to humanity. The moral and spiritual devotion of India is surely one of the greatest of those "good and perfect gifts which come down from the Father of lights."

. . . In my personal religious experience in India I have found the whole perspective of Christian doctrine widening out. It is not possible for me any longer to view human history as one great mistake, one great calamity, with sin in the foreground. Christ came not to destroy, but to fulfill, fulfilling those ages of spiritual striving during which India searched with passionate longing for what is spiritually good. In Jesus of Nazareth's first message in the synagogue there is both healing and construction. It does not imply the pulling down of everything which the saints and sages of India with patient wisdom have erected. Rather it implies the building up of all that is good.

I know that I am open to be misunderstood. Some will at once quote: Christ Jesus came into the world to save sinners. Yes, that is true, vitally true. I hope that in my altered point of view the truth about the sinfulness of sin which I have learned in my earliest years has not become less vital. I can understand the need of probing disease to its root if evil is to be cured, but I see now with far greater clearness that this is not the whole process. Something I did not expect has intervened. The records of the life of Christ in the gospels appear to me more than ever simple, universal. After all these years in India they mould and shape my judgement of men and things and correct my daily life in a way that no other teaching in the world has ever done or could do. They bring me into contact with the great moral realities, they create in me also a longing to get back to simplicity away from what is artificial and conventional.

¤ ¤ ¤

*Andrews emphasizes the goodness of God's creation and refuses to put sin in the foreground of his understanding of Christianity. His faith was inclusive and broadly optimistic. It is interesting that he had to travel so many miles from home and enter into another culture to feel free to be that kind of Christian, for certainly the Anglican tradition could support such an affirmation of the goodness of God. One of the great Anglican teachers of the nineteenth century, in whose path Bishop Westcott followed, was Frederick Denison Maurice. Like Andrews he never denied the reality of sin, but for him it was not the starting point of the Gospel. The starting point is "the absolute love of*

*God; and the reward of the Gospel is the knowledge of that love."*

*Andrews had learned that truth in England, yet he was able to live it out more freely in India when he stepped away from the more conventional forms of Christianity. His teachers in India were many, but it was Tagore who first enabled him, in William Blake's terms, to "cleanse the doors of perception." Tagore's life-affirming poetry led Andrews to re-read the gospels, finding Christ to be one who "enjoyed life to the full in all its finer aspects of beauty and color and form," and whose greatest gift was joy.*

*In South Africa Gandhi became his teacher. Once again he read the New Testament with fresh insight, now discovering Christ's openness and receptiveness to all people of faith, regardless of their race, creed or culture. Yet Gandhi in his asceticism would remind Andrews at times of that world-denying aspect of Christianity he could no longer accept. In many ways Gandhi was too much like St. Paul, Andrews would say, and the New Testament letters of Paul were sometimes hard for him to digest.*

*With St. John, however, Andrews felt completely at home. He was centered spiritually in the upper room of the final chapters of the Gospel of John. In* Christ in the Silence *Andrews tells us that each morning he would meditate on those chapters during the quiet time after the Eucharist, before the day's work began. "Those farewell chapters of St. John's gospel have been like a treasure-house to me in my own life." Along with his many Quaker friends, Andrews could affirm with St.John in his Prologue that Christ is the Light that lightens every person who comes into the world.*

*Gandhi's own witness to the light is compellingly set forth in an address to Christian missionaries at the Calcutta YMCA in 1925. He first speaks humorously of a*

*Christian's attempt to convert him and then tells of the great satisfaction he has found in the* Gita.

¤     ¤     ¤

Not many of you perhaps know that my association with Christians, not Christians so-called but real Christians, dates from 1899, when as a lad I found myself in London; and that association has grown riper as years have rolled on. . . . There was even a time in my life when a very sincere and intimate friend of mine, a great and good Quaker, had designs on me. [laughter] He thought I was too good not to be a Christian. I was sorry to have disappointed him. One missionary friend of mine in South Africa still writes to me and asks me, "How is it with you?" I have always told this friend that so far as I know, it is all well with me. If it was prayer that these friends expected me to make, I was able to tell them that every day the heart-felt prayer within the closed door of my closet went to the Almighty to show me light and give wisdom and courage to follow that light.

. . . Today my position is that though I admire much in Christianity, I am unable to identify myself with orthodox Christianity. I must tell you in all humility that Hinduism as I know it, entirely satisfies my soul, fills my whole being, and I find a solace in the *Bhagavad Gita* and the Upanishads that I miss even in the Sermon on the Mount. Not that I do not prize the ideal presented therein, not that some of the precious teachings in the Sermon on the Mount have not left a deep impression upon me, but I must confess to you that when doubts haunt me, when disappointments stare me in the face, and when I see not one ray of light on the horizon I turn to the *Bhagavad Gita*, and find a verse to comfort me; and I immediately begin to smile in the midst of overwhelming sorrow. My life has been full of external tragedies and if they have not left any visible and indelible effect on me, I owe it to the teaching of the *Bhagavad Gita*.

I have told you all these things in order to make it absolutely clear to you where I stand, so that I may have, if you will, closer touch with you. I must add that I did not stop at studying the Bible and the commentaries and other books on Christianity that my friends placed in my hands; but I said to myself, if I was to find my satisfaction through reasoning, I must study the scriptures of other religions also and make my choice. And I turned to the Koran. I tried to understand what I could of Judaism as distinguished from Christianity. I studied Zoroastrianism and I came to the conclusion that all religions were right, but every one of them imperfect, imperfect natural- ly and necessarily—because they were interpreted with our poor intellects, sometimes with our poor hearts, and more often misinterpreted. In all religions, I found to my grief, that there were various and even contradictory interpretations of some texts, and I said, "Not these things for me. If I want the satisfaction of my soul, I must feel my way. I must wait silently upon God and ask Him to guide me." There is a beautiful verse in Sanskrit which says, "God helps only when man feels utterly helpless and utterly humble."

¤ ¤ ¤

*Gandhi's charge to the Christian missionaries challenges them to abandon conventional attitudes, which saw the Indians as "heathens" and "idolaters," and instead to open themselves to receive all the riches of India. As he speaks it becomes clear that Gandhi is describing someone very like Charlie Andrews, and that the limitations he criticizes belong to those "little systems" Andrews had consciously rejected.*

¤ ¤ ¤

You, the missionaries, come to India thinking that you come to a land of heathens, of idolaters, of men who do not know God. One of the greatest of Christian divines, Bishop Heber, wrote the two lines which have always left a sting with me: "Where every prospect pleases, and man alone is vile."

I wish he had not written them. My own experience in my travels throughout India has been to the contrary. I have gone from one end of the country to the other, without any prejudice, in a relentless search after truth, and I am not able to say that here in this fair land, watered by the great Ganges, the Brahmaputra and the Jumna, man is vile. He is not vile. He is as much a seeker after truth as you and I are, possibly more so.

This reminds me of a French book translated for me by a French friend. It is an account of an imaginary expedition in search of knowledge. One party landed in India and found Truth and God personified, in a little pariah's hut. I tell you there are many such huts belonging to the untouchables where you will certainly find God. They do not reason but they persist in their belief that God is. They depend upon God for his assistance and find it too. There are many stories told throughout the length and breadth of India about these noble untouchables. Vile as some of them may be, there are noblest specimens of humanity in their midst.

But does my experience exhaust itself merely with the untouchables? No. I am here to tell you that there are non-Brahmins, there are Brahmins who are as fine specimens of humanity as you will find in any place on the earth. There are Brahmins today in India who are embodiments of self-sacrifice, godliness, and humility.

. . . I place these facts before you in all humility for the simple reason that you may know this land better, the land to which you have come to serve. You are here to find out the distress of the people of India and remove it. But I hope you are here also in a receptive mood, and, if there is anything that India has to give, you will not stop your ears, you will not close your eyes and steel your hearts, but open up your ears, eyes and, most of all, your hearts to receive all that may be good in this land. I give you my assurance that there is a great deal of good in India.

Do not flatter yourselves with the belief that a mere recital of that celebrated verse in St. John makes a man a Christian. If I have read the Bible correctly, I know many men who have never heard the name of Jesus Christ or have even rejected the official interpretation of Christianity who will, probably, if Jesus came in our midst today in the flesh, be owned by him more than many of us. I therefore ask you to approach the problem before you with open-heartedness and humility.

. . . If you will refuse to see the other side, if you will refuse to understand what India is thinking, then you will deny yourselves the real privilege of service. I have told my missionary friends, "Noble as you are, you have isolated yourselves from the people who you want to serve." I cannot help recalling to you the conversation I related in Darjeeling at the Missionary Language School. Lord Salisbury was waited upon by a deputation of missionaries in connection with China and this deputation wanted protection. I cannot recall the exact words, but give you the purport of the answer Lord Salisbury gave. He said, "Gentlemen, if you want to go to China, to preach the message of Christianity, then do not ask for assistance of temporal power. Go with your lives in your hands and if the people of China want to kill you, imagine that you have been killed in the service of God." Lord Salisbury was right. Christian missionaries come to India under the shadow, or, if you like, under the protection of a temporal power, and it creates an impassable bar.

If you give me statistics that so many orphans have been reclaimed and brought to the Christian faith, I would accept them, but I do not feel convinced thereby that it is your mission. In my opinion, your mission is infinitely superior to that. You want to find men in India and if you want to do that, you will have to go to the lowly cottages not to give them something, but to take something from them. A true friend, as I claim to be of the missionaries of India and the Europeans, I speak to you what I feel from the bottom of my heart. I miss receptiveness, humility, willingness on your part to identify yourselves with the masses of India. I have talked straight from my heart. May it find a response in your heart.

¤   ¤   ¤

*At the end of the address, Gandhi was asked by his listeners, "How do you think the missionaries should identify themselves with the masses?" and his reply was simply, "Copy Charlie Andrews." Later, in a speech to Christian missionary societies in London in 1931, Gandhi spelled out the meaning of that advice in terms of deep affection and respect.*

¤   ¤   ¤

If I want a pattern of the ideal missionary, I should instance C. F. Andrews. If he were here, he would blush for what I want to say. I believe that he is today truer, broader and better for his toleration of the other principal religions of the world. He never speaks with me about conversion to Christianity though we are closest friends. I have many friends, but the friendship between Charlie Andrews and myself is especially deep.

It was love at first sight when I saw him first at Durban. If you asked me whether I have noticed any laxity or indifference about his own fundamental position, I would say that he has become firmer in his own faith and in the growth of love for others. I think, whereas he used to see blemishes in Hinduism, today perhaps he sees those very blemishes in another setting, and therefore becomes more approachable to the Hindu. He is today a potent instrument in influencing the lives of Hindus for the better in hundreds and thousands of cases.

His Indian friends in South Africa wrote to me that he was Deenabandhu—brother of those in distress. He has endeared himself even to the scavenger class, the pariahs. He went to them naturally and influenced their conduct in the simplest manner, and now he is held in very great affection. If I were to compete with him as to which of us had the greatest influence with these people in South Africa, I am not sure that he would not floor me.

¤     ¤     ¤

*When asked in an interview if he had experienced the presence of the living Christ within him, Gandhi's reply was unequivocal. "If it is the historical Jesus, surnamed Christ, that the inquirer refers to, I must say I do not. If it is an adjective signifying one of the names of God—call him Christ, call him Krishna, call him Rama. We have one thousand names to denote God, and if I did not feel the presence of God within me, I see so much of misery and disappointment every day that I would be a raving maniac and my destination would be the Hoogli River."*

*On the subject of conversion Gandhi was equally emphatic, and he and Andrews never saw eye to eye on the subject. Gandhi compared religion to a rose that throws out its attractive scent, drawing us to it, even against our will. We should let our influence on others radiate in the same mysterious way. There must be no compulsion, no attempt at proselytizing.*

*Andrews very much agreed with that, but he remained open to the possibility of a freely chosen conversion to another religion, while Gandhi did not. Gandhi's intransigence here was undoubtedly due to his resistance to colonialism, but he shared that with Andrews. What he did not share with Andrews was his Hindu sense of the importance of heredity. He once put it quite simply: "Believing as I do in the influence of heredity and being born in a Hindu family, I have remained a Hindu." He expected others to remain what they were born to be, whether Christian, Hindu or Muslim. It might also be the case that Gandhi was more sensitive to the danger of communal strife in connection with attempts at conversion. As one commentator has put it, Gandhi saw the status quo in religion as linked to non-violence and peace.*

*In the year 1936 the two friends discussed this issue rather thoroughly, with the following exchange recorded in the pages of Gandhi's paper* Harijan.

ロ　ロ　ロ

C.F.A.: I should like to discuss the fundamental position with you. What would you say to a man who after considerable thought and prayer said that he could not have his peace and salvation except by becoming a Christian?

Gandhi: I would say that if a non-Christian, say, a Hindu, came to a Christian and made that statement, he should ask him to become a good Hindu rather than find goodness in change of faith.

C.F.A.: I cannot in this go the whole length with you, though you know my own position. I discarded the position that there is no salvation except through Christ long ago. But supposing the Oxford Group Movement people changed the life of your son, and he felt like being converted, what would you say?

Gandhi: I would say that the Oxford Group may change the lives of as many as they like, but not their religions. They can draw their attention to the best in their respective religions and change their lives by asking them to live according to them.

There came to me a man, the son of Brahmin parents, who said his reading of your book had led him to embrace Christianity. I asked him if he thought that the religion of his forefathers was wrong. He said, "No." Then I said: "Is there any difficulty about your accepting the Bible as one of the great religious books of the world and Christ as one of the great teachers?" I said to him that you had never through your books asked Indians to take up the Bible and embrace Christianity, and that he has misread your book—unless of course your position is like that of the late Maulana Mahomed Ali's, viz., that a believing Muslim, however bad his life, is better than a good Hindu.

C.F.A.: I do not accept Maulana Mahomed Ali's position at all. I do say that if a person really needs a change of faith I would not stand in his way.

Gandhi: But don't you see that you do not even give him a chance? You do not even cross-examine him. Suppose a Christian came to me and said he was captivated by a reading of the *Bhagavata* and so wanted to declare himself a Hindu, I should say to him: "No. What the *Bhagavata* offers the Bible also offers. You have not yet made the attempt to find it out. Make the attempt and be a good Christian."

C.F.A.: I don't know. If someone earnestly says that he will become a good Christian, I should say, "You may become one," though you know that I have in my own life strongly dissuaded ardent enthusiasts who came to me. I said to them, "Certainly not on my account will you do anything of the kind." But human nature does require a concrete faith.

Gandhi: If a person wants to believe in the Bible, let him say so, but why should he disregard his own religion? This proselytization will mean no peace in the world. Religion is a very personal matter. We should, by living the life according to our light, share the best with one another, thus adding to the sum total of human effort to reach God.

Consider whether you are going to accept the position of mutual toleration or of equality of all religions. My position is that all the great religions are fundamentally equal. We must have the innate respect for other religions as we have for our own. Mind you, not mutual toleration, but equal respect.

◻   ◻   ◻

*In a letter to Gandhi written late in 1936, Andrews articulates his own position clearly. The letter was intended to be the basis for further discussion with Gandhi. It is a confession of his own Christian faith, with the deepest respect for the faith of others, yet with the door to conversion remaining open.*

◻   ◻   ◻

Your talk on religion yesterday distressed me, for its formula, "all religions are equal," did not seem to correspond with history or with my own life and experience. Also your declaration that a man should always remain in the faith in which he was born appeared to be a static conception not in accordance with such a dynamic subject as religion.

Let me take the example of Cardinal Newman. Should he, because he was born in Protestant England, remain a Protestant? Or again, ought I, in my later life, to have remained a rigid Anglo-Catholic, such as I was when I came out to India? You, again, have challenged Hinduism and said, "I cannot remain a Hindu if untouchability is part of it." I honour you for that true statement.

Of course, if conversion meant a denial of any living truth in one's own religion, then we must have nothing to do with it. But I have never taken it in that sense, but rather as the discovery of a new and glorious truth, which one had never seen before and for which one should sacrifice one's whole life. It does mean also, very often, passing from one fellowship to another; and this should never be done lightly, or in haste; but if the new fellowship embodies the glorious new truth in such a way as to make it more living and real and cogent than the old outworn truth, then I should say to the individual, "Go forward; become a member of the new faith which will make your own life more fruitful."

But let me repeat with all emphasis, this does not imply the denial of any religious truth in what went before. It does not mean, for instance, that a Christian is bound to believe that only Christians can be saved, and a Hindu that only Hindus can be saved. My dearest friend, Susil Kumar Rudra, declared openly that he cherished all that was good in Hinduism, and yet he was a profound Christian.

This attitude of Susil's (which has now become my own) is surely in accord with the mind of Jesus Christ. . . . He mortally offended His own village people, among whom He had lived for thirty years, by pointing out to them instances in their own scriptures (such as Naaman the Syrian and the Gentile widow of Zarephath) where God's grace had been found outside the Jewish Church. . . . The Samaritans were outcast by the Jews. So Jesus deliberately takes the Good Samaritan for the center of His parable and contrasts him with the Priest and Levite. When the pagan Roman centurion came to to Him, "I have not found," He said with great joy, "such faith, no, not in Israel." To the Greek Syro-Phoenician woman He said, "O lady, great is thy faith." Not only are abundant examples given of this manner of life which He pursued, but the essence of all His teaching was that God is our Father and that there are no favourites among His children. "He maketh His sun to shine and His rain to fall upon the just and upon the unjust." As far as I can see, He literally went to His crucifixion because he insisted on holding to the full this larger faith.

. . . To repeat, Christ is to me the unique way whereby I have come to God and have found God and I cannot help telling others about it wherever I can do so without any compulsion or undue influence. The Khan Sahib equally holds that Islam is the unique way to God, and I would most gladly sit at his feet, as you and I have both done, in order to find out more and more what Islam means to him; and I would sit at your feet also to find out what Hinduism means to you.

There is a generous phrase of Horace which may almost be translated at sight, "*Maxima debetur pueris reverentia,*" which means, "The greatest reverence is owed to children." Christ said the same thing when He warned us, "See that ye despise not one of these little ones." I feel every day more and more that it is this spirit of reverence that we need—reverence for all that is good wherever it is found.

As far, then, as I can read His life, Christ deliberately broke down every barrier of race and sect and reached out to a universal basis. He regarded His message as embracing the whole human race.

. . . If a living truth is held with all the soul, as you hold it, you cannot help proclaiming it. I honour Paul, the apostle, when he says, "Necessity is laid upon me. Woe is me, if I preach not the Gospel." I recognise in you the same divine necessity, burning within, which makes you say in deed if not in word, "Woe is me, if I preach not that which I hold to be the Gospel."

But then you may answer, "That means we shall always be fighting as to whose 'Gospel' is superior; and this will bring with it all the evils of compassing sea and land to make one proselyte."

I don't think that follows. Let us look at it in this way. I feel, as a devout Christian, that the message which Christ came into the world to proclaim is the most complete and most inspiring that was ever given to man. That is why I am a Christian. As you well know, I owe everything to Christ.

But I readily concede to my dear friend, the Khan Sahib, Abdul Ghaffar Khan, whom I love with all my heart for his goodness, exactly the same right to hold that the message of the Prophet Mohammad is to him the most complete and most inspiring that was ever given to mankind. That is why he is a Muslim.

Since it is to him a living truth, I fully expect him to make it known. He cannot and should not keep it to himself.

And you surely have the abundant right to proclaim to all the world the living truth of Hinduism which you regard as the supreme religion.

I do not think that the act of Christian baptism militates against the idea which I have propounded in this letter, or implies the renunciation of anything that is good in Hindu or Islamic culture. The exact phrase is that we renounce "the world, the flesh and the devil," that is to say, the essential evils of this life. I know that this would imply for a Christian the renunciation of certain things in Hinduism which you would think unobjectionable, such as idolatry, but there are Brahmins who renounce idolatry and yet remain Hindus. I do not want to be loose or vague myself here and I feel that there are clear-cut distinctions between Christians, Hindus, and Muslims which cannot today be overpassed. But I do not think that we need to anathematise one another in consequence. We should rather seek always to see the best in one another, for that is the essential feature of love.

There is a precious element of goodness which we can all hold in common. St. Paul says: "Whatsoever things are true, honest, just, pure, lovely and of good report . . . think on these things, and the God of peace shall be with you."

That seems to me to be a fine way towards peace in religion, without any compromise, syncretism, or toning down of vital distinctions.

I have written this in as objective a manner as possible, when dealing with a subject so charged with emotion as religion is to me. I look forward to the time when the noble phrase of the Qur'an Sharif, "Let there be no compulsion in religion," will be true all over India and throughout the world.

# Chapter 12

## The Final Years

**D**uring the 1930s Andrews continued his travels, visiting South Africa, Rhodesia, and Zanzibar in 1934, with trips to New Zealand, Australia and Fiji in 1936. Increasingly he devoted himself to public lectures and to counseling about the life of prayer, often with young people in universities and schools. But his work for Indian independence and for the welfare of Indians both at home and abroad remained constant.

One example of Andrews' welfare work is his response to the terrible earthquake that took place in Bihar in 1934. While Gandhi visited the victims on location, Andrews set about organizing relief funds in England and South Africa. With respect to independence, Andrews characterized himself as "a propagandist for the development of our moral sense in relation to India." In 1935 he wrote India and Britain: A Moral Challenge, a book which championed Gandhi's vision of self-determination while bluntly opposing the imperialistic vision of British leaders such as

*Winston Churchill, who in a lecture for the B.B.C. had laid claim to India as Britain's continuing possession.*

*Andrew wrote the book in the form of a conversation among Indian students reacting to the Churchill speech. These students were meant to be understood as fictitious personalities, but their words reflect genuine attitudes and emotions that Andrews wanted the English to hear.*

¤ ¤ ¤

When we met again, other students had joined us. One of these was Safdar Ali from St. Jude, a Muhammadan, who was loud in his indignant protest against Mr. Churchill's broadcast. He, like Anil, was a brilliant student who was likely to be a leader in India in the near future. Mulchand, a Hindu from the Punjab, and Abdul Majid, another Moslem, were also present, and their eyes flashed with fire as they declared to me how keenly they had felt the insult and how deeply it had pained them to go on listening to Mr. Churchill. His constant use of the word "Empire" and his mention of India—their own Motherland—as Britain's "possession" had made them furious. His speech had the underlying assumption running through it that their own country belonged to people like him, and they could not bear the thought. His very tone was insulting, as he threw out his racial challenge on the air, little caring that Indians themselves were listening to every word he said.

Abdul Majid told us how, on that night, he had been the guest of an English friend, who had specially invited him to hear this broadcast on India.

"When it was all over," he said, "my friend apologised to me; for he saw what pain I had suffered. But all that night I couldn't get a wink of sleep for thinking about it. It made me wonder if Mr. Churchill realised what young India is thinking today. How would he like it if we talked about *his* country in

185

the same manner? When we hear him, we are inclined to give up all that Mahatma Gandhi has taught us about non-violence and civil resistance. We say to one another, "Brute force is the only thing that an Englishman like him can understand."

¤     ¤     ¤

*There is no question that Churchill understood the power of brute force. His arguments for England's continuing hold upon India were related to England's need to defend herself against Germany:  "Our defences have been neglected. Danger is in the air—yes, I say, in the air! . . .Is this, then, the time to plunge our vast Dependency of India into the melting-pot?" Andrews quotes these words from Churchill's speech and then, in a mocking vein, tell how he had almost hissed the words, "Yes, I say, in the air!" Andrews said it gave him "the creepy feeling of aeroplanes just over one's head."*

*The real danger became evident to Andrews by the time of the Munich crisis of September, 1938, when even he, ordinarily the most peace-loving of souls, acknowledged the need to resist Hitler militarily. Gandhi, however, would have none of that. He was playing quite a different part from that he had assumed as a recruiting agent in World War I. Gandhi said it was the "greater horror" of this impending war that kept him from becoming "the self-ap-pointed recruiting sergeant" he had been before. No doubt his loss of loyalty to the British Empire and the emergency of* swaraj *as his prime political goal were also factors.*

*During these years of the onset of war, Gandhi preached non-violence.  At home he preached unity to a country that seemed bent on division, for the internal conflicts along religious lines were increasing. The burden Gandhi carried within himself as a result of these contradictory forces never seemed to quench his sense of humor or hinder his ability* to make and keep friends. Close friendships such as he enjoyed with Andrews seemed to have the power to sustain him.

Gandhi and Charlie did not work as closely together as they had at previous times, but there were warm visits whenever Andrews came to India. Gandhi would tease his friend about the "wonderful beard" he had grown and then, on a more serious note, advise him to slow down and devote himself to his writing. Andrews had undertaken to write a life of Christ, but he never got very far with it. Should he go to Palestine to write it? he asked Gandhi. No, Gandhi advised, he should write it in India, for it was there that he had found Christ in Eastern form.

Andrews remained permanently in India from 1937 until his death on April 5th, 1940, actively involved with his friends and his causes and spending much time at Tagore's ashram at Santiniketan. When he wrote his will during his final illness, he stated his desire to be buried in Calcutta, near St. Paul's Cathedral, "as a priest of the Christian Church and a minister of the Christian faith." His reconciliation with the church was now complete, even as his identification with India was now permanent.

"Mohan, swaraj is coming," he told his friend when Gandhi visited him in the hospital toward the end of his life. Horace Alexander has in his possession a photograph of Andrews and Gandhi in the hospital room in Calcutta; Gandhi stands by the bedside holding his friend's hand in both his own. It tells the whole story of their friendship, as do their clasped hands—brown enfolding white.

Later on in the course of his illness, after an operation had been decided upon, Gandhi sent him a telegram of support. Andrews read it and remained silent for awhile. Then he said, "I have no anxiety now. . . . Once when Bapu was fasting, I begged him to consult a doctor and he *answered, 'Charlie, don't you believe in God?' I am thinking of that great Doctor today. Whatever he does will be right and good for India and the world."*

*When Andrews died, Gandhi wrote the following tribute in* Harijan.

¤   ¤   ¤

Nobody probably knew Charlie Andrews as well as I did. When we met in South Africa we simply met as brothers and remained as such to the end. There was no distance between us. It was not a friendship between an Englishman and an Indian. It was an unbreakable bond between two seekers and servants. But I am not giving my reminiscences of Andrews, sacred as they are. I want Englishmen and Indians, while the memory of the death of this servant of England and India is still fresh, to give a thought to the legacy he has left for us both. There is not doubt about his love for England being equal to that of the tallest of Englishmen, nor can there be any doubt of his love for India being equal to that of the tallest of Indians.

He said on his bed from which he was never to rise, "Mohan, *swaraj* is coming. Both Englishmen and Indians can make it come, if they will." Andrews was no stranger to the present rulers and most Englishmen whose opinions carry weight. He was known to every politically minded Indian. At the present moment I do not wish to think of English misdeeds. They will be forgotten, but not one of the heroic deeds of Andrews will be forgotten so long as England and India live.

If we really love Andrews' memory, we may not have hate in us for Englishmen, of whom Andrews was among the best and the noblest. It is possible, quite possible, for the best Englishmen and the best Indians to meet together and never to separate till they have evolved a formula acceptable to both. The legacy left by Andrews is worth the effort. That is the thought that rules me while I contemplate the benign face of

Andrews and what innumerable deeds of love he performed so that India may take her independent place among the nations of the earth.

¤ ¤ ¤

*Two years later, Winston Churchill sent Sir Stafford Cripps to India in an attempt to bring Congress into the wartime government. Gandhi had no desire to meet him or to support his mission, but he agreed to see him "for Andrews' sake," as he wrote in a letter to Agatha Harrison. "Sir Stafford Cripps has come and gone. How nice it would have been if he had not come with that dismal mission. I talked to him frankly as a friend, if for nothing else, for Andrews' sake. I told him I was speaking to him with Andrews' spirit as my witness. I made suggestions, but all to no avail."*

*In 1947 Gandhi met with Lord Louis Mountbatten, the last viceroy of India. They were to discuss alternative routes to a united rule in India at a time when Hindu-Muslim divisions appeared to rule out any such possibility. Gandhi asked him if he had ever heard of Charlie Andrews, and then suggested that Mountbatten might take Andrews' place. If he could devote his life to the service of India as Andrews had, Gandhi suggested, Mountbatten might qualify to serve as the head of an Indian state, appointed and salaried by the Indian government. It was one of Gandhi's more quixotic proposals, revealing both his strong feelings for Andrews and his desire for "the best Englishmen and the best Indians" to meet and work together as he and Andrews used to do.*

*So the friendship and what it stood for continued to work on Gandhi's mind as India approached the date set for its independence in 1948. When he ended his final fast on January of 1948, a fast for equitable dealing between the now-divided states of India and Pakistan, the young girls of his entourage sang for him, "When I Survey the Wondrous Cross." He must have thought of Charlie then. A few days later, on January 30th, Gandhi was assassinated. He died with his favorite name for God upon his lips: "Rama."*

It was a film that first prompted me to write this book. Appropriately enough, what will most likely remain with us after reading it are certain images: the face of the frightened coolie or the ecstatic child, the scene of the shower of white garments at Chittagong, Charlie bending down to touch Gandhi's feet. Their writings may well serve as as an impetus for further works in comparative religion or the philosophy of non-violence, but, even more immediately, they serve as illustrations for any reader who is committed to the same goals as Gandhi and Charlie. My hope is that they have the same effect as stories and pictures in the gospels and the Book of Acts do of calling us to a renewed sense of what is possible.

Debates on the main questions these men addressed will continue endlessly. Is it really possible to end the oppression of the poor, and to do so without violence? Can there be mutual respect among the followers of the world's religions? Can the curse of racism and intolerance be lifted? It is hard to make a positive case based on reason and experience alone; faith is an essential ingredient.

The gospels and the Acts of the Apostles do not debate with us very much. Instead, they offer stories and images—some plain, some wondrous, all intended to alter our sense of what is possible. Jesus performs a sign, or tells a tale, and then he admonishes his followers not to be faithless, but believing. His signs and stories are about the reign of God; they call for our response, either by imitation, as in the sacraments, or by making new signs ourselves that point to God's rule in our day.

Gandhi and Andrews were makers of signs. Inspired by their scriptures, they created new images that would illustrate the inner meaning of what their traditions taught. Renunciation, learned from the *Gita*, was made visible by Gandhi in the life of the ashrams, or in discrete acts, such as his changing from formal barrister's attire to the simple dress of the coolie. Charlie's washing of the disciples' feet inspired Andrews' touching of the feet of the Sikh headman who had been abused by his fellow British.

While Gandhi and Andrews could each be impulsive, they also tended to be very careful about the images they presented to their own people. Each had a fine sense of the enacted parable and for the scene that would touch the hearts of those who saw it. For both men, costume was significant: when Andrews changed from *khaddar* to a European suit, it made any words to Congress on the question of burning foreign cloth almost superfluous. The staging of events could be important, too, as we saw in the ceremony carefully planned by Gandhi at the end of the Great Fast.

Each was a critic of what he thought to be the wrong image. That is one reason why Andrews criticized Gandhi severely for literally "playing with fire" in his campaign against foreign cloth. Similarly, when his friend announced his fasts to the death, Andrews wondered uneasily what these fasts would convey about the spirit of non-violence. Gandhi himself used Andrews' criticisms as a mirror of English opinion, a perspective he sorely needed, for he wished to win the English by symbolic communication that they, too, could understand. Yet there came times when what he communicated to Indians mattered most, as in the Epic Fast of September 1932, the fast that touched India's heart but could not be fathomed by the British.

Their friendship itself became the image of a possibility that could never be proven or refuted by argument, by mere words or disagreements. Whenever the component parts of their mutual Hindu-Christian understanding were spelled out, there was always some remainder, something left unreconciled—whether the issue was conversion, or celibacy, or non-violence itself. Yet whenever I look at the photograph given to me by Horace Alexander, showing Andrews in his final illness with Gandhi by his side, I sense the love that bridged those gaps and am myself more ready to risk a friendship beyond the boundaries of my own tradition.

When people saw Gandhi and Charlie together in their lifetime, their obvious love and respect for one another communicated to Indians Gandhi's truth that respect for India's oppressors was still possible. To the English, the friendship spoke of Andrews' truth that false pride and racial supremacy had had their day and now it was time to learn lessons from their subject people.

Andrews' entire way of perceiving reality had been formed by New Testament imagery. He cultivated this way of seeing as he meditated daily on stories from Scripture, especially from the Gospel of John. We have noted how he viewed Gandhi and his movement in a New Testament frame, as when he compared the Phoenix ashram in South Africa to the earliest Christian community pictured in the second chapter of Acts.

I am not qualified to comment on Gandhi's way of seeing except to note that the mythological tales of his tradition were deeply imbedded in his psyche. As a child he was fascinated by the performances of itinerant players dramatizing the story of Raja Harischandra, who gave up crown and kingdom in pursuit of justice and truth. Gandhi's biographers tell us that he wanted to be Raja Harischandra in his own life. Indeed, Gandhi wrote in his mature years that the seeker after Truth (God) must be fearless, like Harischandra. "The story of

Harischandra may be only a parable; but every seeker will bear witness to its truth from personal experience, and therefore that story is more precious than any historical fact."

It is interesting that both these deeply religious men were what we would call "modernists." For example, one of Andrews' difficulties with continuing to function as a priest was that he found it impossible to consent to a belief in the doctrines of the virginity of Mary and the bodily resurrection from the dead. Gandhi wrote, "My belief does not require me to accept every word and every verse in the sacred poems as divinely inspired . . . I decline to be bound by any interpretation, however learned it may be, if it is repugnant to reason or moral sense." It was not literal truth that these two sought in their scriptures, but images and metaphors that would enable them to see life whole and resolve its contradictions in action.

In Gandhi's commentary on the *Gita*, he makes it very clear that it is poetry he is interpreting. He says that just because a poet has a particular truth before the world, it does not mean that he has known or worked out all its consequences, or even that he was able to express them fully. "In this perhaps lies the greatness of the poem and the poet. A poet's meaning is limitless." Andrews himself wrote poetry—not very good poetry, but good enough that we can find there a clue to the meaning of his life as the working out of the implications of those images the gospel writers had set before his eyes.

None of this is to suggest that political and social ends, such as independence and equality, were dissolved by Gandhi and Charlie into some poetic mist. It is rather to say, as Gandhi often did, that ends are always subordinate to means, since no one knows what the end will really be in any case. The means, therefore, are to be carefully chosen. They are to be measured by the degree to which they themselves communicate the truth about the desired ends. We are called upon to model the truth by our actions. What is your message? Gandhi was continually asked. He answered that his life was his message.

The cross is the central image from Christian scripture that provided a meeting point for the two friends. "When I Survey the Wondrous Cross," the hymn Charlie sang for Gandhi in his fasts, expresses the doctrines that bound them together in their work. These were the renunciation of self and the practice of *prayaschitta*, that penance which takes the form of actions intended to set free not only the penitent, but all who observe them from their sins of hatred, pride, or fear.

The contemporary liberation theologian, Aloysius Pieris, looking for the convergence of Hindu and Christian teaching, points out that the Hindu doctrine of renunciation "allows the cross to shine as the supreme locus of Jesus' revelation of the divine." Andrews' most compelling words about the meaning of the cross are in some reflections written during his early journeys in Africa.

> The Gospel of Jesus is an austere Gospel—austere because it mean sacrifice at every turn, sacrifice of wealth, sacrifice of ease, sacrifice of comfort, sacrifice, when the call comes, of life itself. And this life of sacrifice must be undergone not as a cold formal virtue, but as a burning passion.
>
> There is no escape from this appeal of Jesus, and the disciple seeks none. The cross must be taken up, not now and then at our own pleasure, but daily. The yoke can never be wholly removed. Only the joy of service makes the burden lighter, and the following of Jesus makes the yoke more easy to bear. "My yoke," he says, "is easy and my burden light."
>
> This, then, is what it means to be a Christian: not the expression of an outward creed, but rather the living of an inner life.

For Gandhi, the spirit of the cross pervades a mantra he translated from the first verse of the *Ishopanishad*, the mantra he interpreted with his life and with which we will end.

> All this that we see in this great universe
> is pervaded by God.
> Renounce it and enjoy it.

# End Notes

## Introduction

---

p. 3    Gandhi to Alexander in Horace Alexander, *Gandhi through Western Eyes* (Bombay: Asian Publishing House, 1969), p. 203.

p. 5    Gandhi to Andrews in *The Collected Works of Mahatma Gandhi* [henceforth, CW] (The Publications Division, Ministry of Information and Broadcasting, Government of India, 1964) 31:171.

p. 6    Erik Erikson, *Gandhi's Truth* (New York: Norton, 1969), p. 24.

Gandhi to Andrews in CW 15:3-4. "Love at first sight" in CW 48:122. For full text, see p. 175.

# Two Seekers and Servants

p. 8      "Our hearts met" in C. F. Andrews, *What I Owe to Christ* [henceforth WIO] (New York: Abingdon Press, 1932), p. 222. "Two seekers and servants" in CW 71:408.

p. 10      Bishop Westcott's influence is described in C. F. Andrews, *The Inner Life* (London: Hodder and Stoughton, 1939).

pp. 10-11      C. F. Andrews, "Impressions of Gandhi" in *The Gandhi Reader*, ed. Homer A. Jack (Bloomington, IN: Indiana University Press, 1956), pp. 389-91.

pp. 12-14      From "Speech at Quilon" in CW 44:258.

pp. 14-16      M. K. Gandhi, *An Autobiography: The Story of My Experiments with Truth* in CW 39:126-7.

pp. 17-21      WIO, pp. 136-41. For Andrews' conversion experience, see pp. 86-92.

p. 22      "On Reading Gitanjali" from *The Motherland and Other Poems*, quoted in Daniel O'Connor, *The Testimony of C. F. Andrews* (Madras: The Christian Literature Society, 1974), p. 93. For the comparison of Gandhi to St. Paul, see "Impressions of Gandhi."

p. 23      "I saw that nations" in CW 48:434.

# South Africa

p. 24      The edition of *Indian Opinion* quoted here and on p. 27 was kindly made available to me by Dr. Gary Klein.

p. 26    Andrews to Munshi Ram, quoted in Hugh Tinker, *The Ordeal of Love: C. F. Andrews and India* [henceforth, Tinker] (Delhi and New York: Oxford University Press, 1979), p. 79. "The Indian leaders met" in Benasaridas Chaturvedi and Marjorie Sykes, *Charles Freer Andrews: A Narrative* [henceforth, Chaturvedi] (London: George Allen Unwin, 1949), p. 95.

p. 27    Andrews to Tagore in Chaturvedi, p. 98.

p. 28    Gandhi to Manilal in CW 12:340-1.

pp. 29-30   WIO, pp. 235-6.

p. 31    "A Historic Debate" from *Indian Opinion* (17 June 1914); CW 12:431-2.

pp. 32-3   WIO, pp. 222-4.

pp. 34-5   WIO, pp. 217-8.

pp. 35-7   WIO, pp. 215-7.

pp. 37-8   WIO, pp. 229-31.

p. 39    WIO, pp. 221-2.

p. 40    WIO, p. 233.

p. 41    Gandhi to J. E. Andrews in CW 12:542. Andrews to Gandhi in Tinker, p. 90.

# "What I Owe to Christ"

p. 42    For Santiniketan, see WIO, chapter 17.

p. 43    "Emasculated life experience" in a letter to Gandhi, Chaturvedi, p. 110.

pp. 43-4   C. F. Andrews, *India and Britain: A Moral Challenge* (London: SCM Press, 1935), pp. 122-3.

p. 45    WIO, pp. 224-5.

pp. 46-7   WIO, pp. 256-8.

pp. 47-9    WIO, pp. 258-63.

pp. 49-50   "Speech at Ahmedabad Meeting" in CW 14:273.

pp. 50-51   "Significance of Fiji Struggle" in CW 16: 109-10.

pp. 52-3    C. F. Andrews, *Sandhya Meditations* (Madras: G. A. Natesan, 1940), pp. 122-7.

p. 53       "The Indentured Coolie" in Chaturvedi, p. 326.

# Amritsar

pp. 55-6    C. F. Andrews, "Gandhi as a Religious Teacher" in *The Americanization of Gandhi*, ed. Charles Chatfield [henceforth, Chatfield] (New York and London: Garland Publishing, 1976), pp. 372-3.

pp. 56-7    Gandhi to Andrews in CW 14:444.

pp. 57-61   Gandhi to Andrews in CW 14:474-8.

pp. 62-3    Gandhi to Andrews in CW 14:509.

p. 64       Gandhi to Susil Rudra in CW 14:511.

p. 65       Andrews to Gandhi in P. C. Chaudhury, *Gandhi and His Contemporaries* (New Delhi: Sterling Publishers, 1972), p. 50.

pp. 67-9    C. F. Andrews, *Christ in the Silence* (London: Hodder and Stoughton, 1933), pp. 94-96.

pp. 69-71   "Punjab Letter" in CW 16:312-14.

pp. 72-4    CW 16:314-16.

p. 75       C. F. Andrews, *The Sermon on the Mount* (New York: Harper and Brothers, 1962), p. 109.

p. 76       C. F. Andrews, *Sadhu Sundar Singh* (New York and London: Harper and Brothers, 1934), p. 22. The quotation from the Granth Saheb appears on pp. 38-9. The story of encountering the headman appears in Chaturvedi, p. 136.

p. 76     CW 43:82.

# The Oppression of the Poor

p. 78     "Pariah, untouchable" in *Young India*, 17 November 1921.

p. 79     Andrews to Gandhi in Chaturvedi, p. 155. Gandhi's response in Tinker, p. 164. "Independence, complete and perfect" in Chaturvedi, p. 166.

p. 80     "There is room in this resolution" in CW 19:160. The text of Gandhi's resolution was: "The object of the Indian National Congress is the attainment of *swaraj* by the people of India by all legitimate and peaceful means," in CW 19:159.

p. 81     "What is the sum and substance" in *Young India*, quoted by Nicol Macnicol, *C. F. Andrews: Friend of India* (London: J. Clarke, 1945), p. 55. For Andrews' speech, see Chaturvedi, p. 166.

p. 82     For Andrews' presentation of the five goals, see C. F. Andrews, *Mahatma Gandhi's Ideas* [henceforth, *Ideas*] (New York: Macmillan, 1930), p. 319.

pp. 82-4  C. F. Andrews, "Homerule and Homespun" in Chatfield, pp. 301-4.

p. 84     For Andrews' response to reporter, see C. F. Andrews, *The Oppression of the Poor* [henceforth, *Poor*) (Madras: S. Ganesen [1921?]), pp. 119-24.

p. 85    Andrews as "embodiment of peace" in Chaturvedi, p. 172.

pp. 86-8   *Poor*, pp. 1-6.

p. 88    "These children here" in WIO, p. 251.

p. 88    "India has always seen" in *Christ in the Silence*, p. 67.

pp. 89-91   *Poor*, pp. 7-15.

pp. 91-2   *Poor*, pp. 16-18.

pp. 93-4   *Poor*, pp. 66-8.

# Violence or Non-violence?

p. 95    On Tagore's criticisms of Gandhi, see *Ideas*, chapter 15, "The Great Sentinel." "Fully capable of controlling" in George Catlin, *In the Path of Mahatma Gandhi* [henceforth, Catlin] (Chicago: Henry Regnery, 1950), p. 195.

pp. 96-9   *Ideas,* pp. 270-3.

p. 100    "Infinitely beyond" from Andrews to Tagore in Chaturvedi, p. 179. The event near Amritsar is described in Chatfield, pp. 371ff and in Chaturvedi, p. 187.

pp. 101-2   *Ideas*, pp. 257-8.

p. 102    "If we are not to evolve violence" in Catlin, pp. 195-6.

pp. 103-4   "The Great Trial" in CW 23:114-5.

p. 104    "Even C. F. Andrews" in Catlin, p. 199.

# The Gift of Peace

pp. 106-10 From *Atlantic Monthly* (November 1924), pp. 668-71.

p. 111      *The Gospel of Selfless Action, or The Gita according to Gandhi*, by Mahadev Desai, quoted in *Selected Writings of Mahatma Gandhi*, ed. Ronald Duncan (Boston: The Beacon Press, 1951), p. 37.

p. 111      On Gandhi's teaching about "God as poor," see C. F. Andrews, "Gandhi and Indian Reformers" in *The Yale Review* (March 1930) 19:504.

pp. 112-3 *Ideas*, pp. 344-5. "Gitanjali X" may be found in Rabindranath Tagore, *Collected Poems and Plays*( New York: Macmillan, 1965), p. 5.

pp. 113-6 Extracted from chapter one of *The Inner Life* by Marjorie Sykes in *Charles Freer Andrews: Representative Writings* (New Delhi: National Book Trust, 1973), pp. 221-3.

p. 116      Gandhi to Agatha Harrison in Chaturvedi, p. 268.

p. 117      "No continuous, untroubled faith" in Chaturvedi, p. 269.

p. 117      *The Inner Life*, p. 109. Gandhi to Andrews in CW 61:142. Cable in CW 69:20.

p. 118      Gandhi to Andrews in CW 25:38.

# The Great Fast

p. 121      Gandhi to Andrews in CW 25:157.

p. 121      "I have to be very firm indeed . . . . It means
incessant watchfulness, but everyone knows
that it is out of pure love that I am taking up
this responsibility, and they obey me very easily,
while it is probable that they would not obey others."
From letters to Dwijendranath Tagore in Chaturvedi,
p. 207.

pp. 121-2      *Ideas*, pp. 306-7.

pp. 123-5      *Ideas*, pp. 311-13.

p. 125      E. Stanley Jones, "The Soul of Mahatma Gandhi" in
*The World Tomorrow* reprinted in Chatfield, p. 652.

pp. 125-30      *Ideas*, pp. 313-18.

p. 131      "The pathway of love" in *Ideas*, p. *308*.

p. 131      Andrews to Tagore in Tinker, p. 214. Gandhi to
Andrews in CW 25:244.

# Untouchability

pp. 132-4      *Ideas*, pp. 169-71.

p. 134      "*Swaraj* meaningless" in *Young India*, 25 May
1921. "If we fail" in *Harijan*, 5 January 1934.

pp. 135-6      *Ideas*, pp. 179-80.

pp. 136-7      *Ideas*, p. 164.

pp. 137-9      Gandhi to Andrews in CW 19: 288-90.

pp. 139-41 *Ideas*, pp. 165-8.

pp. 141-2  Andrews' sermon in Chaturvedi, pp. 187-8.

p. 143  Andrews to Gandhi in Chaturvedi, p. 263.

p. 143  Andrews to Alexander, 27 December 1929, from the private collection of Horace Alexander.

p. 144  Andrews to Gandhi in Macnicol, p. 67.

# Interpreting Gandhi

p. 145  Andrews to Alexander, December 1929, from the Alexander collection. The three books were *Mahatma Gandhi's Ideas* (1929), *Mahatma Gandhi—His Own Story* (1930), and *Mahatma Gandhi at Work* (1931), all published by Macmillan.

pp. 146-7  Andrews to Gandhi in Chaturvedi, p. 233. Andrews to Gandhi in CW 43:109.

p. 147  "I would far rather" in Tinker, p. 245.

p. 148  Agatha Harrison, "C. F. Andrews" in *Christian Century* (28 September 1932), p. 1168. Gandhi to Andrews in CW 47:47.

p. 149  "The King had enough on" in Louis Fischer, *The Life of Mahatma Gandhi* (New York: Harper & Row, 1983), p. 281.

pp. 150-1  *Christ in the Silence*, pp. 292-3.

pp. 152-3  Harrison, p. 1169.

p. 153  Gandhi to MacDonald in Fischer, p. 306.

p. 154  Cable from Gandhi to Andrews in CW 51:50. Tagore on the Epic Fast in Fischer, p. 311.

pp. 155-6    *Christian Century* (October 1932), pp. 279-81.

pp. 156-7    Andrews to Gandhi in Chaturvedi, p. 264.

pp. 157-8    Gandhi to Andrews in CW 51:345-6.

p. 159    Gandhi to Andrews in CW 52:244-5.

p. 160    Andrews to Lord Allen in Chaturvedi, p. 265. Andrews to Gandhi (cable and response) in CW 55:149-50.

pp. 161-2    Andrews to Alexander in Chaturvedi, p. 273.

p. 163    Gandhi to N. I. Mashruwala (regarding *tapascharya*), in CW 52:169.

p. 163    Gandhi to K. Naoroji in CW 52:269.

pp. 163-4    Andrews to a friend in Chaturvedi, pp. 273-4.

# Religious Truth

pp. 165-6    "Discussion with Missionaries" in CW 34:261-2.

pp. 166-9    C. F. Andrews, "My Quest for Truth" in *Representative Writings*, pp. 216-20.

p. 169    "The absolute love of God," F. D. Maurice to F. J. Hort in Porter, Wolf, eds., *Toward the Recovery of Unity* (New York: Seabury, 1964), p. 145.

p. 170    For Tagore's influence on Andrews, see WIO, chapter 14. The quotation is from p. 206. On the meditative reading of the Gospel of John, see *Christ in the Silence*, p. 56. The quotation is from p. 301.

pp. 171-5    Speech by Gandhi to Christian missionaries in CW 27:434ff.

pp. 175-6    Speech at a conference of missionary societies, in CW 48:122-3.

pp. 176-7　For Gandhi on the names of God, see speech to Christian missionaries above. On religion as a rose, see speech at conference of missionaries above. On heredity, see *Ideas*, p. 359.

p. 177　For Gandhi on the status quo in religion, see J. V. Vilanilam, *Religious Communication in India* (Trivandrum: Kairali Books International, 1987), vol. I:189-90.

pp. 177-9　*Harijan* in CW 64:19-20.

pp. 179-83　*The Guardian* (4 March 1948) reprinted in O'Connor, pp. 118-22.

# The Final Years

pp. 185-6　*India and Britain*, pp. 25-6.

p. 186　"Creepy feeling" in *India and Britain*, pp. 20-21. "Self-appointed recruiting sergeant" in Fischer, p. 344.

p. 187　"Wonderful beard" in Chaturvedi, p. 277. Conversation on the life of Christ in Tinker, p. 291. Description of last days, Chaturvedi, pp. 317-8.

pp. 188-9　"Legacy of C. F. Andrews" in CW 71:408-9.

p. 189　Gandhi to Harrison in CW 76:60-1. Conversation with Mountbatten in Tinker, p. 314.

p. 192　On Gandhi and Harischandra, see Fischer, p. 302.

p. 193　"The story of Harischandra" in Duncan, p. 49. "My belief does not require" in Vilanilam, p. 190. "In this perhaps lies the greatness" in Duncan, p. 40.

p. 194　See the discussion of Gandhi's life as message in Vilanilam, p. 196. Aloysius Pieris, SJ, *An Asian*

*Theology of Liberation* (Maryknoll, NY: Orbis Books, 1988), p. 64.

p. 195    C. F. Andrews, *Christ and Labour* (London: SCM, 1924), p. 123.

# Index

The royalties from the sale of this book will be donated to the Bishop Desmond Tutu Southern African Refugee Scholarship Fund. This fund enables young people who have been forced to flee South Africa because of their opposition to apartheid to attend colleges in the United States. It is administered by the Phelps Stokes Fund, 10 E. 87th Street, New York, NY 10128.

Archbishop Desmond Tutu clearly stands in the tradition of C.F. Andrews within the Anglican Communion, having devoted his life to the struggle against racism. Andrews would have rejoiced to see his day, and would be pleased with any project that aids students, for they were among his greatest loves.

Gandhi once said to the Corporation of the City of Delhi, which was preparing to honor Andrews for his work, that it would be a cruelty to give him money, for "he is not a monied man. He has almost literally nowhere to lay his hand on. He has no cupboard, no treasure chest, no house of his own. He never keeps anything for himself . . . But if the Corporation would spend any money it would be proper to vote a purse for him to be used for his life mission." The proceeds from this book are offered as a contribution to the continuation of that mission.

¤    ¤    ¤

This book is printed on acid-free paper and was manufactured in the United States of America.